Praise for
The Family on Beartown Road

"Cohen has written a frank, funny and unexploitative memoir. . . . It's hard not to be charmed by her simple, straightforward style."

—*The New York Times Book Review*

"A triumphant epic of coping." —*The Boston Globe*

"Cohen's amazing reserve of humor and honesty in the face of adversity . . . recall such classics of domestic perseverance as Anne Lamott's *Operating Instructions*." —*Time*

"A touching memoir . . . What makes the book so sympathetic is Cohen's lack of self-pity and the straightforward tone. . . . [A] superb chronicle." —*People*

"A healing journey . . . a potent articulation of the ties between one generation and the next." —*The Washington Post Book World*

"Cohen's book is . . . a fascinating exploration and mapping of the human mind's trajectory over the course of a life." —*Elle*

"Cohen blends a journalist's straight-talk style with a novelist's skill in imagery and timing. . . . [She] finds poetry and beauty in the quotidian." —*The Seattle Times*

"Beautifully written and moving, this compelling memoir will be enjoyed by all readers." —*Library Journal*

"An important source of support and comfort for those struggling with the emotional turmoil associated with tending a sick loved one." —*Psychology Today*

D1468666

"The book is poignant and sad, funny and real, and highlights what is universally nutty about living with other people."

—Melissa Fay Greene,
author of *The Temple Bombing* and *Praying for Sheetrock*

"Its strength lies in its power to inspire hope. Alzheimer's is a dreadful disease, but Cohen shows there is beauty in its depths."

—*Oakland Tribune*

"Cohen writes a lyrical, simple and unsentimental prose. . . . A warm, triumphant and high-style memoir."

—*Milwaukee Journal Sentinel*

"Cohen . . . captures the irrepressibility of a young child and the poignancy of a man nearing the end of his life in an incredibly touching story that examines aging and family responsibility."

—*Booklist*

"By turns harrowing and funny, sweet and sad. It ultimately leaves the reader with not only a greater understanding of the extreme pressures family care-taking causes for individuals . . . but also of the positive, even joyous outcomes that such circumstances present." —*Albuquerque Journal*

"The adventure and peril of everyday living captured in language that's light, beautiful, and razor-sharp."

—*Kirkus Reviews* (starred review)

"Moving yet unsentimental . . . Cohen's fluid prose lifts her forceful story to a higher level, making it a tribute to her father and her family." —*Publishers Weekly*

PHOTO: Maureen Ryan

ELIZABETH COHEN is a reporter and columnist with the Bing-hamton *Press & Sun-Bulletin*. She has written for *The New York Times, Rolling Stone, Family Circle, Parenting, The New York Times Magazine, Newsweek,* and other publications. With Lori Alvord, she is the author of *The Scalpel and the Silver Bear.* Elizabeth and her family live in Port Crane, New York.

The
Family on
Beartown Road

The
Family on
Beartown Road

A Memoir of Learning and Forgetting

Elizabeth Cohen

Originally published as *The House on Beartown Road*

 Random House Trade Paperbacks

New York

2004 Random House Trade Paperback Edition

Copyright © 2003 by Elizabeth Cohen
Author interview copyright © 2004 by Random House, Inc.

All rights reserved under International and Pan-American Copyright Conventions. Published in the United States by Random House Trade Paperbacks, an imprint of The Random House Publishing Group, a division of Random House, Inc., New York, and simultaneously in Canada by Random House of Canada Limited, Toronto.

RANDOM HOUSE TRADE PAPERBACKS and colophon are registered trademarks of Random House, Inc.

This work was orginally published in hardcover as *The House on Beartown Road* by Random House, an imprint of The Random House Publishing Group, a division of Random House, Inc., in 2003.

Grateful acknowledgment is made to BOA Editions, Ltd., for permission to reprint an excerpt from "The Statues" from *Yannis Ritsos: Selected Poems, 1938–1988* by Yannis Ritsos, translated by Minas Savvas, edited by Kimon Friar and Kostas Myrsiades, copyright © 1989 by BOA Editions, Ltd. Reprinted by permission of BOA Editions, Ltd.

Library of Congress Cataloging-in-Publication Data
Cohen, Elizabeth.
    The family on Beartown road: a memoir of learning and forgetting / by Elizabeth Cohen.
    p.   cm.
    ISBN 0-8129-6663-5 (pbk.)
    1. Cohen, Elizabeth. 2. Cohen, Sanford, 1920—Mental health.
3. Alzheimer's disease—Patients—Home care—New York (State)—Binghamton. 4. Caregivers—New York (State)—Binghamton—Biography. 5. Mothers—New York (State)—Binghamton—Biography. 6. Alzheimer's disease—Patients—New York (State)—Binghamton—Family relationships. I. Title.

RC523.2.V36 2003
362.1'96831'00974775—dc21   2002036758

Random House website address: www.atrandom.com

Printed in the United States of America

9 8 7 6 5 4 3 2 1

Book design by Mercedes Everett

For Daddy and Ava
and in remembrance
of Julia Catherine Cohen

Contents

viii • Contents

Prologue

0–40–80

Those were our ages the year my father came to live with my baby and me. We span time neatly—add forty to each of our ages and arrive at the age of the next. There was something about our circumstances over the course of that year that seemed choreographed, as if to make a point.

This is the story about how our three lives came together for a time in rural New York. It is also the story about the human mind in three of its stages. My daughter's learning curve was a near vertical incline. She began to grasp the most subtle insinuations; she did not miss a single sliver of light falling on the living room floor nor fail to greet one without an expression of surprise and her characteristic "Hi!" or kiss. It seemed she learned new words and then phrases by the hour, then began stringing them together into things that resembled sentences. Then she acquired the beginnings of real speech, with all the subtleties of tone and language.

My father, at the opposite end of the parabola, seemed almost sievelike, leaking words, ideas, concepts, and feelings. He would grow tongue-tied and fumble for the names of things and people. A proud man, masculine in the way that is common for those of his generation, he was at first embarrassed to ask for help. He would talk around the gaps, make up for missing words with other words. But the shame was soon overcome by the fear of not knowing. Then the questioning became incessant. He wanted a map of the world, with instructions for all things.

My daughter was a typical baby, learning things at exactly the pace the textbooks predict. My father was diagnosed with mid-to-late-stage Alzheimer's disease, a malady that I would learn affects more than 4 million Americans and is poised to claim a shocking 14 million by the year 2020. It robs him daily of what he knows, what he loves, and what he has experienced. And it is robbing us of him as he transforms little by little, from a person who knows us to one who does not.

During the time this was written I lived in between these two people at life's two poles—in every sense. The child of one, the parent of the other, caretaker of both, I lived in the small space between their needs, between the snowy and, later, lush green confines of the front and back yards of our house, between learning and forgetting.

Just like my age, my cognitive abilities seemed to be set dead center between theirs. I began to notice how I learn things. I began to notice, also, how many things I forget. I came to feel I was trapped there in the midlife of the mind, recognizing each day what a bright country I had come from and what a dim one might lie ahead.

I celebrated all my daughter's firsts. Likewise, I had to mourn all my father's losses. There were numerous coincidences. She said "Mama" on the same day he first asked me who I was. She said "Baby Aba"—her name is Ava—the same week we received our census and my father looked for a long time at the form before asking me his own name.

Our situation, connected by blood, by memory, and by circumstance, gave rise to the most shining example I have ever seen of the human mind's course, as it winds through the territory of a life.

The
Family on
Beartown Road

chapter 1

Dream Detection

————⟨⟨∞ ❊ ∞⟩⟩————

Sometimes at night I lie awake for hours beside my baby daughter, Ava, cupping her head in my hand. Maybe I am imagining, but sometimes I swear I can feel it: I can feel her dreaming. The sensation upon my fingers is less than a vibration but more than stillness. A something-in-between-nothing-and-something, vague but true. I imagine I can feel my daughter's mind becoming.

Touching her head in this way comes naturally to me, an instinctual rather than a conscious act. I do it because I am afraid of our circumstances as winter approaches. And because I understand now how delicate a mind is, the many ways in which it can fail a person.

When I was a child, whenever I felt upset, overwhelmed, unsure of my actions or that my thoughts were racing too fast to catch them, I developed the habit of placing my hand on my forehead. It has a calming effect, as though in doing so I can actually slow my mind down, fully possess it, or redirect its course.

Just as I touch my daughter's head, at times when I wake from a particularly vivid dream, I have found myself cupping my own forehead. My hand on my head seems to help me better recall my dreams, as if it is an umbilicus from the sleeping world to waking, a bridge.

Just when I feel my daughter's dreams begin to swirl inside my palms, she often twitches or smiles or mumbles things that are not quite words but that, judging from her expressions, are sometimes serious, sometimes amusing. That is my favorite thing—when she laughs in her sleep. Never at any time—not when I first held her, wet and new, not when I comforted her when she was teething, not even when I fed her by breast—have I felt as close to my daughter as I do when I touch her dreams.

Down the hall from where we sleep lies my father. I know when he dreams, too, because in his sleep he shouts and whimpers, declares and rages. He begs for my mother. He pleads. He shakes the bed. His dreaming is very busy.

Yet listening to him I have this thought—that if I were to place a hand upon his forehead I would not feel a thing. There would be no subtle almost-vibration, no activity within that brain that once graded reams of undergraduate term papers, lectured about abuses of migratory laborers, charted trends in factory employment and union membership. That mind that once won him a fellowship to Harvard to study industrial relations would be startlingly silent. I fear that touching the forehead of my father, a professor emeritus of economics, I would feel nothing. Rather than signs of a mind's activity, his dreams seem like echoes of a past intelligence. His voice in the night is a habit, a reflex. He calls out because he can. That is all.

The baby dreaming beside me is acquiring all the cognitive

processes that will guide her in life. My father has Alzheimer's disease; time, place, people, and events all blur and dissemble for him. It has stolen almost all of his connections to life.

Just as I have considered the mechanics of dreaming, I have begun to think about thinking. Thinking about thought is a peculiar experience. When it is someone else's thought it is mostly conjecture, because no person is privy to that most private space of another. When it is my own thought it is confusing and sometimes scary. I can detect both the strengths and the flaws in my mind, its laziness and gaps and the great trough of forgetting that opens between certain events. And it occurs to me, when I sense this canyon of lost memories snaking through my life, that I hate forgetting. I hate it more than anything—sorrow, indifference, hunger, cold. It takes and takes, a robber who absconds with ideas, names, dates, prized moments, song lyrics, stanzas of poetry, recipes, the punch lines of jokes. It steals what a person truly owns; it takes the life he has lived, leaving him stranded on the island of the present.

Forgetting is my only real enemy. And it is taking my father in fits and starts, in chunks and in slices, stretching out the pain of loss unbearably.

But forgetting lives in our house now like another person. It is always hungry. I go into my husband Shane's painting studio, where the canvases sing with color and seem so immune to erasure, and I wonder—when will it encroach here? Someday will he forget the way cadmium meshes with black, the lovely moment of approaching a freshly gessoed canvas, the way he spits on his fingers and rubs the chalky color from pastels into a muted shadow on a face?

I watch myself forgetting to pick up toothpaste when I am

shopping, forgetting to give my father his medication, forgetting the date, forgetting the capital of Tennessee. It is insidious.

My daughter does not yet know enough to forget. Each thing in her mind is a bright new resident, firmly affixed and special. She remembers where the cookies are, gets excited when I approach the jar. She points at a carton of chocolate milk on the left side of the refrigerator behind the juice. She is just beginning to approach speech; still, she communicates remembering very well. While we are surprised that she can remember so much, she is nonchalant. She has been alive under a year, yet she acts like she has always known these things. For Ava, remembering comes naturally, like a sneeze, a hiccup.

She is learning so fast now that I cannot keep up with all she knows. She is learning her body. Not with words, but locations. Say "nose," and sometimes, I swear, she points at her nose. Say "tongue" and out hers pops. Did I teach her the location of her tongue? When did I do that? I rack my brain for a recollection of an instance of tongue instruction, but none comes to me. If I did, I have forgotten it. But she hasn't.

One recent night as I lay beside her, watching her laugh at some secret amusement as she slept, my father walked into the room. He saw me there, touching her head while her subconscious laughter pealed forth. I waited for him to comment, to say something about her laughter, about my hand on her laughter, about her beauty, there on the pillow, a mass of dark curls spread out around her face. Instead he seemed embarrassed, as though he had walked in on a private moment. As though her joyful sleep were something intimate he should not have seen.

"Look," I said, inviting him into her beauty. "She laughs in her sleep."

He walked over and glanced down, looking at Ava laughing and sleeping.

"You know," he said, considering her, "I was thinking about that same thing recently. That funny thing. But now it's gone."

chapter 2

Before

⟶ ⟨⟨◇◇⟩⟩ ⟶

Not so long ago we were just a family, like any family. We lived in New York City. I worked as a reporter at the *New York Post* and also wrote stories, essays, articles, and the occasional poem at a desk in the corner of our bedroom while Shane painted in the living room. The day our daughter was born, we walked the four blocks from our apartment to the hospital. Twenty-four hours later we returned, rolling Ava along in a stroller. One day we were two people, the next day we became three.

The following summer we strapped our daughter into a Snugli and took her to street fairs, parks, Indian restaurants, and an island off Greece. We saw all the other families, with their new babies, looking like us, doing what we were doing. Being a family like other families, doing family sorts of things, was a good feeling. It felt right.

I met my husband, Shane, in 1995 in the tiny town of Gallup, New Mexico, where I was living then. I first saw him at a party. It was instant. We moved toward each other and then stayed there. It was the easiest thing. There wasn't even anything resembling a date. We met and then were. It didn't require discussion.

I fell in love with his sense of humor, the whimsy and intelligence in his paintings that filled a loft in a storefront on the main street of town. I fell in love with the smell of his shirts. It was weeks before we revealed even the most introductory information about each other. By then, it was too late.

Shane is fifteen years younger and, by society's standards, entirely inappropriate for me. When we met, he'd assumed I was younger and I thought he was older. We liked the same music, food, books, and movies. We both liked to get in our cars and drive, straight into nowhere, without destinations or maps. We ventured into forests and canyons, through Navajo country, where the wind sculpts rocks into whimsical forms, and onto the Zuni reservation, where the broken hills are striped red and white with mineral deposits. Within two years we were married and moving to New York City to pursue our careers in writing and art.

But when we had our daughter, Ava, two years later, it was suddenly important to us to get back to a rural place, like the one where we had met. New Mexico seemed too far from New York City, so we started driving on weekends through New York State, Pennsylvania, Connecticut, and New Jersey, looking for newspapers where I could work and real estate where we might live. When we saw the old farmhouse on Beartown Road, near a medium-size paper that had offered me a job, it seemed destined.

It is a small white house, floating on the top of a hill in a sea of lilacs and hydrangea. It has creaking floors and leaded windows and a generous porch with two chairs on which we imagined spending long, lazy summer afternoons, drinking iced tea and reading novels. It has a tree for a swing, two more trees perfectly spaced for a hammock, and a huge loft space for Shane's paintings. It is a simple house, farmer-built. There is nothing fancy about it, but it is solid—a place where you think things will go right, people will love each other, and children will grow up happy and healthy. From the minute we walked through the rooms we knew it was for us. All of us.

Our family seemed to increase every day. The cats came to us on their own as cats do. First came Lulu, found in the rain in Manhattan before we moved; then, six months after we arrived came Milo, a long noodle of a cat who slips out of your arms as though oiled, a gift from Samme Chittum, a fellow journalist and friend, who had made the same career trek from Manhattan to the Binghamton paper; Twyla—later to be nicknamed Twytwy—turned up one day on our front porch. Soon after came the dalmatians, Samo and Franny—a sister and brother we bought from the Shumachers, breeders down on Tunnel Road.

Life seemed idyllic. The world of my own childhood, of nightly slipping between clean, sun-dried sheets, having dined on meals made from my mother's favorite recipes, pressed between pages of her dog-eared copy of *The Joy of Cooking,* was repeating, in my life.

Night was a time of dark sugar, safe and sweet. My family curled inside it, myself between the warm bodies of my husband and baby, my father's shredding brain over a thousand miles away. From time to time, as we slept, someone would roll over and toss an appendage somewhere over someone else. My husband's arm would wrap around my waist. The baby would fling a leg over my arm. She tucks her toes beneath me the way I used to tuck my toes beneath my sister when we were small and slept together. And she breathes like my husband, in short, irregular snores.

I didn't know how sacred that sweetness was, nor fathom how quickly it could disappear. I had no clue how disaster could smack into a life and change everything.

But it did. It hit, and night and everything else would never be the same.

Daddy came to live with us in the sticky heat of August. I got the phone call from my sister, Melanie, late in the summer of 1999. Earlier that year Melanie had moved with her two children into my parents' home in New Mexico. It had become clear by then that something was wrong. My father was not himself. And my mother, whose health was failing, was not able to care for him alone.

We'd noticed the creeping changes in him for some time. After several fender benders, and fearful of his declining driving skills, my sister and mother convinced him to turn over the car keys in 1997. It was a battle. He got really mad, insisting that after fifty years he was a better driver than ever. But in the end he acquiesced. I believe he recognized that he had become dangerous behind the wheel.

No one dared say the word. We circumvented it daily, the way you might avoid a homeless person raging in the subway. We mastered the euphemism. We said things like "mixed up," "confused," "spacey," and finally "unsettled" to describe him during those nights he walked from room to room, opening and shutting closet doors.

The house my mother had always kept antiseptic-clean and pin-neat had begun to swirl in papers and opened files. Clothes were strewn over the floor, drawers left open. Things were getting lost more and more frequently. His yellow urine stains could not be scrubbed out of the carpets near the bathroom, no matter what my mother tried. Caring for both of them, each with their own needs, was more than my sister—a single working mother—could handle.

What's more, my sister told me Mommy and Daddy were fighting—horrible shouting matches that ended with my mother in tears. "I don't want my kids to hear it," my sister said. "It's awful, she screams at him and throws things. Then he gets mad and yells back. She keeps calling him stupid."

That was the first moment his disease became real to me. Before my sister told me about my parents' fights, it had been fuzzy—an *if*, a *perhaps*. In an instant it grew a shape. It became a thing, but a terribly unknowable thing, like a black hole in space. My parents were not the sort of parents who fought. They'd always agreed on everything. That my mother would ever call my father stupid was inconceivable.

They say black holes are invisible but that people know they are there because of their effect on the things around them, the way they chew up stars and galaxies. I knew Daddy's disease was real because of the way it was consuming our world, the people around him. My mother.

She had always worshiped my father and, in fact, had tended the hearth of his intelligence almost professionally for decades. She had typed the books he wrote. She filed, she annotated, she whited-out. She edited, rubber-banded, and paper-clipped his intelligence. She gave up her own jobs, as an administrator, a grant writer, a teacher, a potter, to be his assistant, his behind-the-scenes helper. This change in him, from brilliant to befuddled, defied everything she knew. "Stupid, stupid, stupid!" she yelled at him several times a day.

Stupid was a strange word to hear from our mother. We were not stupid. We didn't know people who were stupid. We didn't call people stupid. It was foreign, a piece of linguistic shrapnel that had no place in our lives.

Our house had always been an intelligent house. Our family walked around inside it knowing things. The way some families play touch football or ski together, we exchanged facts. My mother's passion was crossword puzzles. From time to time she'd shout out queries, like "What was Jean Valjean's resort?"

From another room in the house, two or three of us would yell back, "Sewer."

"Creator of Mrs. Sarah Battle?"

"Lamb."

"No, starts with E."

"Elia," Daddy would say. "His pen name."

He knew the hard ones. That she had taken to calling him stupid was unfathomable.

"I can't take care of both of them," my sister said in that fateful phone call.

"Please, please," she asked, "take Daddy."

Take Daddy.

It was a request that I, like so many adult children, had never anticipated—to "take" one's parent. Especially my father, my fiercely opinionated, intellectual father.

My parents are not the sort of people one imagines taking

anywhere. They took themselves places. To London and New York in theater season; to Russia, Sweden, and Norway on cruises; to St. Croix in the winter; to the annual economic conventions where my father would give presentations before the leaders of multinational corporations. They took themselves to their favorite places, like the Golden Nugget, in downtown Las Vegas, where Daddy played low-stakes blackjack all night and my mother played the nickel slot machines. My parents went there every year, sometimes more than once. They knew the name of the chef.

In fact, in my experience, it was my father who took *us* places. He took the whole family on his sabbaticals and teaching assignments abroad. We'd lived in Venezuela, Bolivia, and Puerto Rico. He'd taken me to Israel with him, to a conference on international labor relations, when I was thirteen, and to field hockey practice when I was in high school. When I was in college at the University of New Mexico, where he taught, he used to take me to lunch at the Faculty Club, where a man named Gus would grill us hamburgers over charcoal.

You don't "take" my father. He takes you.

But not taking Daddy was an even more inconceivable thing to consider. What was the alternative? My sister said she couldn't handle living with both my parents. My mother had agreed.

"Take him," she reiterated.

"Of course," I said. Of course I would.

Daddy had come to all my ice-skating and ballet and piano recitals when I was little and clapped even though I was dreadful. He whispered my lines to me when I played Christopher Robin in the Albuquerque Children's Theater production of *Winnie-the-Pooh*. He brought my sister and me dolls from all over the world, Thailand, Kenya, Japan. And he'd always been good for a double pat on the back (but not hugs or kisses, he was not demonstrative that way) when I'd needed one.

To turn him away was impossible. So we took Daddy.

I discussed it with Shane. We were up for it, we made plans. We were even getting excited. We would give him Ava's room at the end of the hall and move her into the smaller room near us. Then he would have the view out twin windows down Beartown Road of the valley that filled every morning with mist. We would get a subscription to *The New York Times* and *The New Yorker,* his two favorite things to read. We would cook brisket, we'd stock the kitchen with rye bread and pastrami. We'd get better mustard.

After all, we had only one child and there were two of us. My job as a journalist wasn't quite as demanding as my sister's job in telecommunications. I could wear jeans to work; she had to put on suits and stockings every day. And we had this house we'd just bought, with more than five acres in the rural country-side of Broome County, New York. We took Daddy because it felt like the right thing to do. The good thing.

I had no idea.

chapter 3

The History of Love

>———⊰⟨✦ II ✦⟩⊱———<

Ever since I can remember, my parents were in love. Their love was its own country. It had pastures and mountains and valleys and streams. Each day they walked through it, marveling at its beauty. They were the kind of parents who kissed.

Julia and Sanford Cohen. Their love was a busy thing. It was public, and it had plans. They would frequently talk all night long, in excited voices, about politics, education, economics. But mostly they talked about each other. The second marriage for my father and the third for my mother, they could not get over their enormous luck in finding each other. When we went to restaurants, they picked tables where they could sit side by side and hold hands. Sometimes they embarrassed us. They'd peck or hug at parent-teacher meetings at our school, in open view of our friends. They looked lovingly at each other in airports, as though they had just met after long separations. My sister and I lived on the periphery of their great, lucky love. It was not that they didn't love us, too—they did—but we fit in around the edges and corners of their feelings for each other.

My mother told me at an early age that they had children because "it was the thing to do then." Other people were having children, so they did. But once we arrived, full-blown humans, with cuts and pimples and dentist appointments, I think they were sort of flummoxed. They never failed to attend to our needs and undertook the most formal route of parenting, with private schools and piano lessons, conversational French and summer music camps. But it was an effort. My mother seemed incredibly drained by it. It took her away from my father's side, from attending to him, her life's work.

I always had the feeling my mother was burdened by my very presence as a child. That somehow, just by being, I was distracting her from something important she needed to do. When I was sick, it seemed to annoy her. When I accomplished something, she would take a deep breath as though preparing herself for the task of congratulating me.

She often lost her temper completely. Both my sister and I recall the dreaded hairbrush that she used to spank us. It was never a planned punishment, but rather a spur-of-the-moment thing, usually wielded when we talked back to her. I remember that sometimes, when I really thought I deserved, as she put it, "a good smack," I would not get one. Then out of the blue, if something I said was interpreted as "fresh," one would come, swift and stinging. There was a mystery to it. I would wait for my mother to tell my father about it when he came home from work. I waited to hear her version of the important punishment event that occurred in his absence. She rarely did. When he got home, a door seemed to open to her real life. She quickly put the contents of the other life out of her mind.

If I ever reminded her I knew her secret, that she wasn't really enthusiastic about her mother role, she would wait until my father came home and then begin to cry. She would let him coddle her and talk sternly to us. I always appealed to my father's sense of fairness. But there was no fair arbitration to be had when it came to my mother. He would listen to other sides, but he doggedly stood up for her. It was frustrating, because there was another person there who would have weighed the words spoken and brokered peace as he did in the outside world. But in the case of my mother, there was no diplomacy, no fair hearing. It was cut-and-dry. "Be nicer to your mother," he'd say. "Go apologize."

And so I have apologized to my mother all my life. I still do it today, out of habit. Whenever she takes offense at some small thing and cries or gets upset, I say I am sorry. I do it for my father, as though he could still order it, as though his instructing voice were right at my back. But it isn't, and my mother knows it. She is beginning to see that she is on her own. I think it must be terrifying for her.

When my father's mind began to loosen its grasp on the world, my mother's love quickened. It grew wings and teeth and extra hands. As he lost abilities, she seamlessly took them on, absorbing the responsibility for all the things he was failing to do. It exhausted her, but she didn't say anything to anyone. She became stoic. She made do.

Their lucky love, too, was changing, forcing them into a landscape of alienation and isolation. To my parents, whose entire life journeys had been predicated on the constancy of the known, such an unknowable state was not unsettling, it was devastating. Panic became a fellow traveler. My mother felt deceived. How could my father have something—even a problem—she did not have? How could he go so far away without her? It was unthinkable.

My father's intellect had defined him as a man. It also defined him as a husband. The loss of Daddy's mental acuity was confounding to my mother. If he no longer knew who he was, who was she? What then, when he no longer knew her? It was beyond unthinkable. It was an abomination.

Bringing Daddy to live with our family seemed necessary to all of us. When my sister called and told of us of Daddy's decline and Mommy's inability to cope with it, we'd thought, What better place for him than with us, his family, with our animals and nature? Shane flew out to New Mexico and drove back with him in Daddy's blue 1985 Volkswagen Jetta, which was covered in dents and dings, souvenirs from the last days of his driving career. One door had had a handle knocked off. Another was not openable. The car was like a map of his decline, dent by dent. Daddy brought a few suitcases. The rest of his belongings were boxed up and sent on separately.

I do not know what it was like for my mother the day Daddy left. She did not tell me, and I did not ask.

For a time things seemed calm as we settled into our new life with Daddy. Shane dug a pit in the backyard and we grilled hot dogs and hamburgers over coals. We went on long drives down country lanes and sang to amuse Ava, which seemed to work out well for Daddy, too, who chimed right in, remembering most of the words to "The Itsy-Bitsy Spider" and "Old McDonald Had a Farm." Ava sang along with the "E-I-E-I-O" part. Every time she uttered it, Daddy would say, "How about that!"

But the house on Beartown Road, it turned out, was not the solution for Shane. While I worked as a reporter at Binghamton's daily newspaper, covering the night police beat and local events, he had agreed to be a stay-at-home dad. With

Daddy's arrival, the stay-at-home job became increasingly difficult. Ava was learning to walk and had a particular attraction to the steep staircase, and Daddy asked questions all day long: Where is Mother? What is my job? Where is my money? How much money do I have?

"Excuse me," Daddy would politely say, "but could you please inform me of the whereabouts of my wallet, my passport, and the most direct route to Cleveland?"

By the twelfth round each day, Shane had had enough.

The house on Beartown Road, too, was far from the buzz of life in New York: friends, all-night diners, galleries, museums, and pot dealers who deliver ounces faster than you can get a pizza. Too far also from the red hills of New Mexico. Shane had hiked those hills every day. He began painting them obsessively, along with wistful cityscapes, on huge canvases in the Beartown Road studio.

Nine weeks after Daddy arrived, Shane decided to leave us. He said he had to go because I was angry too much. And because it was so stressful, taking care of Daddy and Ava.

"I'm not happy," he said.

And so, late in October 1999, twelve days after Ava's first birthday, Shane took eight hundred dollars and our 1987 Jeep Cherokee and drove back to Gallup.

The morning he left, the trees were burning with autumnal gold and there was a hint of frost icing the grass. Daddy, Ava, and I stood on the front porch and watched him drive away. The baby said, "Bye-bye, bye-bye, Da," and opened and closed her fist backward to wave, the way babies do.

When we went back inside, Daddy asked me where Shane was going.

"Gallup, New Mexico," I said.

"That is a long trip. Does he have enough money?"

"I think so. He has about eight hundred dollars."

"That should do it," Daddy said. Then, pausing: "Who is he, anyway?"

"He is my husband," I said.

chapter 4

The Beginning of Memory

————◦◦)(◦◦————

S uddenly, the world is dangerous. The trees wave their dying leaves in the wind like red flags, as if to say, "Warning."

I try to heed, to preempt disaster. I start with signs.

Taking black markers, I make cue cards, instruct with directions. I try to think of everything. I write BATHROOM side by side with a drawing (crude, I admit) of a toilet. For the hallway and stairs, more signs with arrows. To get outside, two arrows: one pointing down, one right, toward the front door. What if there were a fire? Such signs could save his life.

I gesture and say, "Daddy, this is the way to the bathroom."

"Oh, right, right, this way." He walks into the laundry room.

"No, over here." I physically orient him. "See here. This sign tells you."

"Clever," Daddy says. "You thought of that?"

"Yeah, pretty good, right?"

"Brilliant."

Daddy can be sarcastic sometimes, wry, subtle, a master of the double entendre. But is this sarcasm? I want it to be. But I cannot tell for sure.

I walk him nightly to his room, which I have labeled with a sign that says SANDY, short for his given name, Sanford, and hand him his pajamas. On his dresser I have placed three pictures: one of Melanie, from her high school prom; one of him standing in a soldier's uniform beside his brother, Sol; and one of me, when I was eight years old, that had been on the desk of his office for years. I hang another, of him and my mother, on the wall. I want him to feel familiarity in this room. I am hoping that he will eventually come to recognize it as his.

In the beginning, it was Shane who changed his clothes and prepared him for bed each night. Now I do it. I pull down the sheets and blankets and watch him get in. Then, I pull the covers over his shoulders. If I do not do this he will sleep on top of the bedding or beneath the thin top coverlet, cold and uncomfortable, all night long. I learned this when I went to wake him one morning and found him lying in a fetal position, shivering, with nothing over him but a shirt.

After he's in bed, I put Ava down to sleep. I read her stories from her books: *Good Night, Sleep Tight, Roosevelt Rhino; Fluffy Bunny;* and *Goodnight Moon.* From the time she was about eleven months old, she has insisted on only these three books before she goes to sleep. She has learned the sounds of certain words and phrases in them. She recognizes elements in the pictures, like when Roosevelt Rhino takes a bath in his book. Ava loves baths. When we get to that page, she always perks up.

The other night, when I was midsentence, she announced, "Bubble!" Roosevelt had taken a bubble bath, her favorite kind.

He also has a yellow plastic duck, like she does. On another day she chimed in with a little ambient noise: "Quack, quack!" Sometimes she says, "Quack, quack," before we even turn to the page with the duck.

She is anticipating. She is remembering.

She makes me wonder when remembering begins, just as now I am forced to consider when, exactly, it ends. I am sure that there are academics who have studied this, measuring response time to certain stimuli and so forth. But I wonder when the memory of feelings starts, like love. I think Ava began feeling love the moment she saw our faces, Shane and me, standing over her in the nursery at Beth Israel Medical Center in Manhattan. She blinked hard, and although the baby books say it happens much later, I could swear she smiled. And ever since then, our faces, in pictures or in real life, are her home. So in my own anecdotal way, I suppose I am asserting that memory begins just after birth, when a child sees its parents for the first time.

Sometimes I wish I believed that remembering could come later, because there are things in our lives now I would rather Ava forget. There is a page in the story of Roosevelt Rhino that has been worrying me particularly, when Roosevelt's parents come up to say good night and his daddy's slippers "tip the broken stair." I always skip that part now. I don't want to make her more aware than necessary of our new daddyless circumstances. When I sing her "Hush, Little Baby," I have edited the line "Daddy's gonna buy you a mockingbird" to "Pop-pop's gonna buy you a mockingbird." Pop-pop is what she calls my father.

Sometimes I put Ava to bed first and Daddy helps me get her down. He sits beside her while I rub her tiny baby back.

Once I asked him if he could remember the soldier story, one he made up, which was my favorite from childhood. "How does it go?" he asked.

"It starts out, 'The war had ended,' " I said. " 'A soldier was on his way home alone.' "

"Oh right, right, right," he said. He ceremoniously cleared his throat. And then he said the words: "The war had ended. A soldier was on his way home alone. He was passing through many countries. He went through the country of snow, the country of daisies, the country of delicious potatoes, and the country of very, very tall trees."

We both sat silently for a moment, appreciating his accomplishment, as though he had just remembered the specifics of the theory of relativity. How many times must he have recited those words all those years ago? The soldier story was still there. The beginning was all he remembered, but it was enough. Ava had already fallen asleep.

Tuck-tuck. Night-night. Little baby goes to sleep tonight.

Mornings are my biggest challenge. Dressing Ava and Daddy and myself, feeding everyone, walking the dogs, feeding them, feeding the cats, and straightening up just in time for one last diaper change exhaust me. By the time we leave I feel ready for bed.

I know they don't mean to, but Daddy and Ava make it even harder. I put scrambled eggs on Daddy's plate and on a plate on the tray of Ava's high chair.

"Okay everyone, dig in," I say.

He picks up his knife and begins to cut the eggs and then proceeds to try to levitate them into his mouth with the knife, a complicated maneuver that fails completely. Meanwhile Ava grabs a fistful of her eggs and flings them across the room, where they adhere to the wall.

"She's thrusting food out! She's thrusting in here," Daddy calls to me in the kitchen, while still trying to pick up eggs with his knife.

"Ava, stop that," I say.

"No."

"Ava, eat your eggs."

"No."

"Daddy, use your fork."

"Right, yes. Which one?"

"The one by your plate. Ava, stop that. I will take your eggs away."

"Way," she says, and then throws the entire plastic plate of eggs onto the floor.

"Oh my God," says Daddy, getting up.

"It's okay, Daddy. It's okay."

I put a few diced sections of an orange on her high-chair tray and she pops them into her mouth. Then I sit down by my father. I show him the fork. "This one."

"Oh, that one. I wondered about that."

"Yes, this is the one you can count on for most eating, Daddy."

The baby laughs and spits an orange at him.

"For!"

I turn to look at her. She just said "fork." Like so many things that come out of her mouth now, it is a word she has never said before. I realize she is helping me teach him the meaning of a fork, a thing she had not yet learned herself until this moment.

"He is a handful, isn't he?" Daddy says.

"Yes. But we have decided to keep her anyway."

Daddy smiles. He may not know Ava's gender, but he understands jokes. He makes them, too. I think that a sense of humor must be hidden in a box very deep in the brain, where diseases have to search for it. Maybe this is an evolutionary tactic, to keep people going.

Before I leave for work, I position Daddy on the couch with newspapers and magazines and an assortment of snacks. I would turn on the television, but Daddy recently informed me that it upsets him. That the only things he likes are tennis and golf. There is no tennis, or golf, in the morning.

I take Ava to her part-time day care and arrange for a baby-sitter afterward. Finding care for Daddy is harder. That I haven't figured out yet. There is no section in the Yellow Pages for elder care, the way there is for child care. Or maybe I am not searching correctly. I look under elder help, Alzheimer help, elder sitters, adult care, any euphemism I can think of. Nada. So I've been leaving him home alone during the day and calling to check in. About half of the time he answers the phone. The rest of the time I worry.

"Daddy," I say, "no matter what, unless the house is on fire, do not go outside."

"Right, right," he says, nodding. "That would not be a good idea." He looks wistful.

"Very bad. I mean, I guess you can sit on the porch, but do not walk off the porch."

"Okay. No off the porch. One more thing."

"What?"

"Can I have one of those smoking mechanisms? Before you go."

I take Ava to the car and strap her in the car seat with her bottle and stuffed bunny rabbit. Then I come back in and light my father's cigarette.

"Now, this," he says, gesturing at his cigarette, "this is what I have been waiting for all year."

The smoke curls and loops and fills a corner of the room. The smoke and the morning sunlight mingle and dance. Ava waits patiently in the car with her toys. I will be late for work. I stand in the doorway while Daddy puffs and exhales like a condemned man, smoking his last cigarette.

He wants me to know he loves things. A cigarette, a cup of sugared dark coffee, a walk in the dusk, a buttered roll. It must be a hard roll, preferably with salt or poppy seeds on it. Not a mushy, factory-produced roll. He may not be able to remember the names of the things he loves, but he can still distinguish between them.

He is a discriminating eater, a discerning dresser—preferring tweed to wool, cotton to polyester. He loves a sunset, especially the kind when the sun gets red and fat and lolls on the horizon. I get him a set of golf clubs at a yard sale, and he picks them up one by one and weighs them in his hands, feigning strokes.

"No, these aren't right," he says, flipping them upside down to examine their wooden heads. "These aren't the good kind."

I know nothing about golf clubs, but he does. He competed in golf and tennis in college. He swam. Sixty years ago he won prizes and scholarship money to Ohio State University for his athletic prowess. Now he can't remember the name of a fork. Yet here is the thing: He knows the difference between a good fork and a bad one. Once I remind him that a fork is a fork, he wants me to know right away that he doesn't find the fork I have handed him a very nice fork. He is right. The forks we use have plastic handles. I bought them at a dollar store. They are cheap.

This is important to him, that I recognize his good taste. Once I remind him how to use a fork, a spoon, a napkin, the location of the arms in his jacket, he is instantly an expert. He decides that he will pass on the knowledge, as well as the power of discriminating. The person he has chosen to pass these on to is Ava. He will demonstrate good fork manners to a baby who is still struggling with fork usage. He will teach her. So every day now he sits beside her; she shows him which utensil is the fork, and then he shows her the right way to use it. "Like this," he says, showing her the proper way to cut meat. "Just like this."

"Fooo," she says, "foo, foo, foo," and offers a poor imitation.

"No, no, no," he says. He is firm but patient. He takes her small hands in his and shows her the way to cut, back and forth, with the knife. "Like this!"

"Foo!" she says.

"We generally don't give babies knives, Daddy," I say. He frowns.

The part of him that can do things expands in her presence. Around her, he is a person who knows things, who can do things. She drinks from sippy cups and an occasional bottle, which he remarks upon. "You can use these," he says, showing her the way to drink from a glass. "You sip, you sip, just like this."

I watch them and try not to smile. They prove every day that I was right about it, this arrangement. It is good he came here. There is a dance they do together that no other two people could do. It is the waltz of learning. A two-step. She, then he; he, then she. Back and forth, showing, doing.

Learning and forgetting are not so different, really. There is a pattern to the way they happen. In both there is powerful emotion, the sense of recognition, the sense of loss.

For him, remembering and knowing leads to something that is almost arrogance. He knows he knows things. He sees that she does not. And he knows he can teach her.

The lessons begin. It is their job, their game. It is what they do together.

"No!" Ava says, when he tries to take a bite out of a bar of soap atop the kitchen sink. He looks at it, a white-with-blue-flecks brand meant for serious scrubbing. Then he remembers.

"Come here," he says to her, picking her up and placing her on a chair beside him before the running tap. "Do it like this," he says. He wets their hands and they wash together, scrubbing up to their elbows in bubbles. "This is how to wash." She giggles and tries to touch bubbles with her tongue. She loves bubbles. She is beginning to love him.

In their dance I feel left out, a little purposeless. If he will teach her and she him, what is my job? Then I remember. I am the one who will clean up afterward. I wipe up all the cups they spill. I retrieve the forks they inevitably drop on the floor, the soap that, despite all talk about proper washing etiquette, somehow ends up in the freezer.

My daughter and I are discovering what our roles are to be in this new configuration, with Daddy, without Shane. And Daddy is discovering what his role is to be also.

Only there is one problem: He is changing.

I am not sure about this, but he seems ever-so-slightly more confused than a week ago, and just slightly more confused than he was a week before that. Maybe that is why it is so poignant, watching him teach her things. "This is the way we wipe," he says. "This is the way we put on socks."

Every morning I dress her and hand him his clothing. Then I wait. I want to give him a chance to remember. To keep his dignity. Sometimes I can feel him bristle when I have to help him. And I am so pleased and proud when he remembers, the way I feel when Ava says a new word. There is something about socks and shoes that become rote, akin to chewing and breathing. He can put them on without thinking. He can still button. He can zip. Zipping is coming in handy, too, since there is a distinct draft in the air now, especially in the mornings. A chill has invaded the hills of central New York and we have begun to wear jackets. Some mornings the car windows are latticed with frost. We can see our breath.

There are clumps of bright yellow and red leaves in certain spots on the trees. Other branches are already bare. What makes a certain leaf do that—go yellow before the others and fall? What combination of factors brings that on? There is always one that leads the pack, changing from green, leaving the rest behind.

Ava and I kiss Daddy good-bye in the mornings and wave as we drive away. I adjust the mirror so I can see her in the backseat, singing to herself and blowing him more kisses as we slip over the hill.

chapter 5

Whack

—————⟨⟨∞H∞⟩⟩—————

This is my life now: I currently reside with my father, Sanford Cohen, my daughter, Ava Lilith Van Pelt, two dogs, Samo and Franny, and three cats, in this old farmhouse on Beartown Road in a town that is either named Colesville, Harpursville, Tunnel, Port Crane, or Sanitaria Springs, depending on who you ask. Our deed says we live in Tunnel, we are in the Harpursville school district, our mail comes to the Port Crane post office. Go figure.

A neighbor told me that the name of the road is an accurate description, that there really are black bears living in the vicinity but that I would probably never see one. Sometimes I imagine them, the invisible bears, watching us from secret places where they are preparing for hibernation. Did they see the dogs chase and catch a small rabbit they tore apart on the back lawn, leaving it in bloody shreds? Do they watch the cats flit through the bushes or push through the tiny window in Ava's room and go out onto the roof? Maybe they see her, learning to walk now, and my father, following behind, bent over, helping her. Or maybe they watch me watching over them all. The mama bear.

The invisible bears must know the truth, what nobody else knows, what I hide. That each day arches numerous times toward disaster. That I try to set it back on track as best I can. Sometimes not very well at all.

The idea of bears here, on Beartown Road, is pleasant. They are my gentle, nonjudging neighbors. I consider them my friends. I think of them now, because our isolation is suddenly kind of scary and I need to believe in a benevolent someone nearby. The house is the last house on the road, surrounded by fields overgrown with tall brown weeds. We are miles from the nearest convenience store. We are far, too, from the volunteer fire department and at least twenty-five minutes from the nearest real town, with streetlights and police stations. Our actual neighbors are sparse and merely acquaintances. Some of them raise horses, others have dairy cows. On windy days you can smell the sharp scent of ripe manure, in waves.

At first, after Shane left, I heard every squeak in the house, every wind-slammed door. Sometimes I imagined murderers and robbers plotting to break in, things I never even thought of before. Then I began to hear silences. That was even worse. The silences were gaps in sensory information. They gave me too much time to think about what could be going wrong. That is, until I decided that the bears were out there, watching over us. That thought of them provided peace of mind. Maybe they consider us part of this hill, part of their world. That thought has helped dissolve the fear, for now.

Daddy helps dissolve fear, too, surprisingly. Whenever I am most depressed he says something that makes sense. A little thing. He tells me he thinks the weather is clearing up, or asks me to put on his favorite Frank Sinatra CD. "Old Blue Eyes. That's the one."

Sometimes he even veers toward brilliance, and he's funny. One morning he tells me: "This mother racket you've got going here isn't bad, is it? Especially for us nonmothers."

When I was helping him find the bathroom, I reassured him. "The floor plan of this house can be confusing."

"Confusing squared," he said, then, tapping his head: "Plus, as you may have noticed, I just don't have the same noggin I used to."

Although he may seem it to my mother, or to the casual on-looker, or even to the bears, my father is nowhere close to dim. Even with his brain dissolving, with his neurons pulling apart at the seams, he is smarter than most people I know. In his prime he could strike down an illogical argument with the same swift-ness that you could bat a fly, in one deft stroke.

I never read his books. Not even the first edition of *Labor in the United States*—a heavy tome, thick with facts, which makes an excellent doorstop in a pinch. I have never read them, be-cause I can't understand them. I did try, out of daughterly obli-gation, on numerous occasions, but after four or five pages I always got sleepy.

Just as I stopped trying to read his books, I eventually stopped trying to argue with him, because I could not win. When I was a teenager we'd fight about the West Bank of Israel, the atomic bomb, the importance of education, the Vietnam War, the legalization of marijuana. He outsmarted me every time, catching me in logic traps; I always ended up contradict-ing myself.

It was a waste of time, arguing with Daddy.

For a while after he first came to our house on Beartown Road, when I cautiously brought up his increasing memory loss he said that he didn't believe it. No doctor had ever told him he had Alzheimer's, he said. He called it Alzenheimer's, enunciating the "heim" with a throaty German accent.

Where was the proof?

After just a few days of living upstairs—where he'd bump his head each morning on the sloping eaves of the ceiling—he told me he'd been collecting some evidence and had developed a theory: "I know everybody thinks I have this Alzenheimer's, but there's the reason I am so out of whack—right there."

He gestured at the steep slope in his room, marred by smudge marks where he'd bumped his head. "I get clonked there every day."

He loses things: his shoes, his wallet, his belts.

Strangely, he also finds things. He found a half-read book I misplaced months ago. He found my spare keys.

And he has an eerie predilection for making observations that have credence. He was the one who said the baby, who has mastered the art of turbo-crawling, would fall down the stairs.

When it happens I hear it from the bathroom, where I am brushing my teeth. It sounds like someone hammering: *bang, bang, bang, bang, bang.*

But it is not hammering. It is Ava, tumbling head over heels, banging each stair until she hits, face-first, on the landing and erupts in screams. It is just luck that she is not hurt badly. Nothing broken, nothing even bruised. Babies are sort of elastic and bouncy. They fall well.

Daddy and I rush to comfort and examine her, and Ava flies

into his arms, peering at me from there like a traitor. Somehow I have caused this and she knows it. "Owchy, owchy," she says.

"Is he okay?" my father asks as I examine her on the sofa, giving her magic mommy kisses.

"She's fine, she's fine," I answer.

"Are you sure?"

"Fine. She's fine."

Ava howls.

I am trying to convince myself she is fine. And not just her. I am trying to convince myself that we are fine, too. That I am wrong about the creeping feeling lurking in the recesses of my mind that we are in trouble, big-time. I want so much to believe that it doesn't matter that Shane is gone. That I am not compromised, wounded, or different. That I can take care of everyone, alone.

The truth is we are not okay. Numerous potential disasters loom. Ava finds a bottle of Clorox left uncapped. Daddy drops scissors onto his foot. I feel every moment that safely passes is one more calamity dodged. In every cabinet, in every drawer, around every corner, and in each moment, accidents wait to be set in motion. But I get there just in time; I wrestle away the Clorox, I put the scissors in the very back of a utility drawer.

Daddy and Ava share a propensity for trouble. They both trip, they spill, they both pull reams of toilet paper off the roll and leave it all lying in a looped pile the cats adore.

When you have a baby you have to baby-proof your house, with covers for outlets, with special plastic devices that lock the drawers. But nobody ever tells you how to Alzheimer's-proof your house. You would have to empty it completely. You would have to start from scratch. You would have to reinvent your life.

I wouldn't know where to begin. Right now I am doing all I can, spinning between the needs of these two human beings. It has been a month since Shane left, and still I do not have a system. It is play by play, moment by moment. Disaster by disaster.

Small things constantly go wrong. I mess up. I leave Daddy in an inside-out shirt. I leave Ava a little longer than I should in a dirty diaper. I burn food. I forget to help him brush his teeth or to wipe a smear of ketchup off her cheek. And I feel a new tug in my chest when I look at my daughter. She is getting such short shrift, such a tiny portion of me. It is dawning on me that this is a crappy deal for her.

Other evenings, when I come home from work having written an article that will be in the next day's paper, when I have everyone fed, bathed, pajamaed, and toothbrushed, when the questions have been answered and the stories told, and we are all sitting in the living room together by a fire Daddy and I have built, I feel a surge of success warm me. I am competent. I. Can. Do. This.

I have conquered the enemy. I have won.

Score:
Elizabeth - 1
Alzheimer's - 0

Only then do I take a moment for myself. I take a tiny little slice of time, the way you might cut yourself a piece of rich, chocolatey cake. I make my own observations, for my own self-indulgent reasons. I might admire a mahogany-colored curl on the back of Ava's neck. I might sip my coffee and really taste it. I might look at my father and remember him as he was. That other time. When he was the one who knew things.

I am discovering that babies and old men have a lot in common. Both thrive on routine. They both struggle to find the arms of shirts after you put them over their heads. They both try to put their shoes on while standing and lose their balance. They both respond well to choices. If you use generalities, ask them, for example, if they want to eat something but don't say what, they both say no. But if you give them a choice between toast or pancakes, they pick.

In his own way, Daddy participates in our lives. Sitting on the living room couch, he turns the pages of the newspaper, making an important crackling noise. He doesn't fold them back in order; they end up on the floor in a heap that the baby and cats like to crawl underneath and play peekaboo.

The house fills with the sounds of them, her singsong baby talk, his constant questions about the whereabouts of his wallet, glasses, and wife. They skirt language in opposite directions. Daddy mixes fragments of words together to make new ones. Ava, speaking in almost-words, a sloppy protospeech, dances at language's doorway. The sounds of them combine with the whimpering of dogs, crying cats, and an old house creaking with the weather. It is early November and already snow and sleet pelt the windowpanes regularly. One loose pane upstairs rattles incessantly in the slightest wind. This is our special music, full of staccato and hum.

And there is another sound, a night sound I am getting used to, something moving down the stairs, too big to be a cat. Too careful to be a lumberous dog. It scares me until I discover it is my father. He has taken to walking around the house at about two in the morning once or twice a week.

All his life he trafficked in the academic world of desks and tests, graded hundreds upon hundreds of term papers, shelved thousands of books, shuffled important documents from one place to another. And filed. He and my mother filed away deeds, titles, and insurance claims. At work, he filed facts and statistics. He could pull one from his hat whenever needed: the gross national product of Venezuela, the population of Uruguay, the precise economic status of women in cottage industries in the highlands of Bolivia, the number of union employees on assembly lines in the Midwest.

Out of force of habit, he gravitates to paper. Now, in the center of night, he goes through the things on my desk. He slides framed pictures from one place to another, he reorders the bills, he shuffles through the paper detritus of my life. He empties drawers.

Sometimes when he goes downstairs, he sees the dogs pushing against the confines of the crate they sleep in, anticipating their release to the yard. Three times now, when I have come down in the morning, the dogs have been let out—which would be nice, if he'd simply opened the crate door. Instead, he completely disassembles the crate. He takes the metal stakes out of the sides until the whole thing collapses in pieces on the floor. I can imagine how long this must take and how hard it must be, as well as how frustrated the dogs must get while he does it. A simple latch on the front is something he cannot learn, he cannot remember, although I have shown him each time how to pull it out and swing open the metal door.

Whenever Daddy roams the house and I am not in the immediate vicinity, he takes things apart. He removes the batteries from the television remote, he takes the shelves out of the refrigerator and stove, he unplugs lamps and phones. It is as though, in trying to use a thing, he must thoroughly explore it and understand each component. Or maybe he is just groping. A fraction of a person moving through a whole world, he must reduce it to fractions, like himself.

I have begun to hide things of importance. My wallet, keys, money. Items I will need come morning. Everything else, I figure, will turn up sooner or later, in one spot or another. I found a photograph of my mother in his sock drawer, a Mexican coin under his mattress, my daughter's birth certificate folded neatly in his left sneaker, beneath his driver's license.

I think that maybe, when we are asleep, he comes down at night to play at life. Trying to be as he was before, when he did things, instead of stultifying in the present, when he cannot. Whenever I hear him down there, I go to check on him, and sometimes, like last night, I find him occupied with a task.

"Hi, Daddy," I said. He was eating ice cream from the carton and playing with Ava's Curious George puzzle. He was trying to fit the piece with Curious George on a bicycle into the spot designated for Curious George in the car. Over and over he tried to fit it in, at one angle and then another. "What are you doing?" I asked.

He quickly pushed Curious George with the bicycle behind a sweater that was heaped on the table. "Nothing. Can't sleep, too much noisy rain."

"Why don't you go on to bed, Daddy? It's late."

"Okay. I will. But I can't say much good will come of it."

He got up and walked into the laundry room. "The stairs are right over here," I said, pointing. "Your room is to the left."

"I know. I'll go up there soon."

I went back to bed, listening to the sound of him walking around some more, moving things. Next to me the baby moaned and turned over, her knees beneath her and her rear end sticking up in the air in a position I have come to call the baked turkey. In her sleep she sucked furiously on a pink pacifier, while she clutched another one in her hand.

Fortunately, she didn't cry out for a bottle or sit bolt upright and say, "Mama!"—a new late-night habit of hers. I moved the dog's paw so that it stopped touching her foot and couldn't wake her. Lately, I have taken to bringing Samo—the better behaved of the two puppies—in to sleep with us while his sister Franny stays downstairs in the crate. The book on the care of dalmatians said it is okay, even good, to crate their breed at night, but I hate it. It feels like I am jailing them, and their growing bodies seem so cramped in the tight metal space. Being allowed to sleep with us makes Samo slavishly grateful and well behaved. Still he dreams, like a person, and I was afraid he would have one of his running dreams in which his legs move furiously.

In the morning I am awakened by her, crawling over my back on her way to kiss the dog, the first thing she does every day. When we go downstairs to breakfast I find Curious George with the balloons in the freezer, the carton of ice cream in a cabinet in a sea of melted goop. The flavor is called Super Bowl Sundae and it contains nuts, caramel, and marshmallows. The nuts and marshmallows—usually the prizes my father digs for in each bowl—protrude from the goopy mess in abundance. Scraping them off the wood takes about twenty minutes, during which the baby manages to feed Franny her left patent leather shoe.

My father walks into the kitchen. "I want to ask you a few questions," he says.

The first one: "Exactly who owns that baby?"

chapter 6

Luck and Evidence

>————◄(◦◦}{◦◦)►————◄

When I think about it, there was evidence long ago.

Here is a memory: 1975, Albuquerque. My father is driving us to school in his secondhand turquoise-blue Ford Falcon. It is standard, four gears, on the steering column. He drives very slowly. He brakes more than most people do, jolting the car. He takes us some days for doughnuts at Northdale Plaza on Fourth Street. Daddy has a chocolate-glazed cruller, Melanie has a chocolate cake doughnut, and I have a jelly doughnut. We all have milk in little cartons. We drink from their spouts, that way we won't get milk mustaches. We are happy.

When we get back in the car, my sister and I ask Daddy to put on the radio to our favorite station. We are hoping that "Roundabout," our favorite song by the band Yes, will come on, which it frequently does. It is a long song, ideal for our plot. My sister and I are perfectly silent. We try not to giggle.

My father hums to the song and drives. He goes up Fourth Street, left on Osuna Road, then takes a right on Second Avenue. He hums and drives. We sit in the back trying not to make a peep. We almost hold our breath. We force ourselves not to giggle.

Most days when we do this, Daddy will drive all the way to work at the university. He will pull up in the parking lot behind his office and get out of the car. Then he will see us.

"Jesus Christ!" he will shout. "I forgot to drop you off! Why didn't you say something?"

We suppress waves of laughter rising in us. "We forgot, too, Daddy," Melanie sings out. "We were just listening to the radio."

After the fifth time this happens, Daddy makes a rule: no radio in the car on the way to school, and one girl has to sit in front, where he can see her.

As an adult, from a separate life, in a separate city in the 1990s, I customarily called my parents once or twice a month. Starting in the mid-nineties, the time it took for phone calls to be answered began to lengthen. From two rings to four, and then to five or more. Although I knew my parents were almost always at home, that my father's business relationships and almost every one of their friendships had all but faded away, the answering machine would often pick up. It gave the comforting impression that they were busy people, always out.

Since my father ran his arbitration business from home, it had long been his practice to be the one to answer the telephone, not by saying hello but with the single word "Cohen."

Even after he retired, after he stopped arbitrating, after he ran no business out of the house, he would answer that way: "Cohen."

I'd always made fun of it; it seemed so stiff and formal and somehow incomplete as a greeting. I took to answering back: "Cohen too."

But then came a time when my sister and I noticed he would answer and other things happened. There would be the sound of fumbling and then the sound of him pushing buttons. As though he were dialing, strangely, and the numeric melody sounded like it was our home phone number. It was as though, from the moment he picked up the phone to the single next moment, he'd forgotten that he was answering rather than making a call.

When he did speak he would say, "Anybody there, hello, hello?" and then, finally, "Cohen."

Sometimes when the phone was answered, there would be silence or the sound of my parents speaking to each other.

My mother: "Push that button, there."

My father: "Which button? This one?"

The phone would disconnect. Or sometimes you could hear them arguing.

My mother: "It's upside down, turn it over."

My father: "Where?"

My mother: "Like this."

Fumbling sounds, buttons being pushed. Often the answering machine would engage. Sometimes she would yell at him: "Hand it to me. Just hand it to me!"

My father: "Here, take it!"

More sound of buttons being pushed. Finally, his voice. "Cohen."

"Daddy, Daddy, Daddy. It's me."

Then came the day when he spoke back, saying: "Who?"

"Beth."

"Beth who?"

"Cohen."

A pause, then me again: "I mean, Cohen, too."

And he laughed then. Remembering. But he had lost me for a moment. I had slipped away.

That is what I mean by evidence.

Now, in the house on Beartown Road, when the phone rings Daddy starts opening doors, entering rooms, searching for it. He gets upset, starts looking in drawers. He answers the door. He goes outside. One day, when it rang, he began searching frantically through his wallet.

When the phone rings, Ava gets excited, too, frantic; running around, reaching for the receiver when I answer, as though somehow the call might be for her. At thirteen months old, she has become obsessed with telephones. I often find her playing alone with the cordless, speaking into it. Over and over she says the two clearest words in her current idiom: "Hi! Hi! Hi!" and "Bye-bye."

She loves the act of dialing—I think all babies do—and then she puts the phone to her mouth and talks and talks, saying hi to Mommy, to kitties, to Big Bird and Elmo from *Sesame Street*.

Once she actually called someone. They live in South Dakota and apparently had a conversation with Ava: On the bill the call was listed as two and a half minutes long.

I buy her a toy phone, which she plays with for approximately six minutes before establishing that it isn't the real thing. She sees right through it, with its musical messages, barking dog, and mewing cat. She thinks it is fine for the car but makes it clear that in the house she wants AT&T or nothing.

For the short time she did play with the toy phone, when she pushed the Ring button, it was Daddy who was fooled. He'd go for the real phone. He picked it up and pushed buttons. He spoke over the dial tone: "Hello, hello, hello. Cohen."

Then Shane calls from Gallup. Ava and Daddy sit staring at me as I answer, as if they know. Their eyes are too inquiring, they can tell by my face. The phone has brought unsettling news into our world. I walk into the other room.

He says he wants to talk. He misses us. How are we?

I can't think of any sentence to fill the void following the question. Instead, I leave air, an expensive silence that ticks away. How are we?

"Sometimes we are great," I say.

We get through meals and baths and mornings. We are still here. Ava has no father in her life. That is how we are.

I pass the phone to Ava, who has pushed open the door. She starts dancing with happiness, hearing his name. A jumping-up-and-down dance, a grabbing and twirling dance.

"Da! Hi!" she says. She gives the phone a peck and hugs it to her chest, and when I try to pry it away she screeches and then cleverly disconnects us.

For a moment I think he is coming back. Maybe he is already on the way, calling from Oklahoma or Pennsylvania. Lessons have been learned, apologies will be made. There will be gifts and kisses and a small sore spot between us, like a bruise you keep rubbing to see if it has gone away yet.

But he doesn't call back. Not that night or in the morning, either. Still, hope has ignited us. I can see it in Ava. And in me.

For days I wait for the follow-up call. The call when it will be my turn to ask questions, to say I am sorry, to hear him say so, too. But it doesn't come.

I have begun to hate the phone, how it sits so smug on its little table, how it doesn't ring. Shane found that table discarded on the streets of New York. What a find, that little fifties table. How lucky we thought we were then.

Lucky, in fact, is how I have often felt. Lucky to be me. Lucky to be the daughter of my parents, so brilliant and interesting. Lucky to travel with them all over the world. Lucky to live in the rambling house they bought in Albuquerque when I was in the seventh grade. So many lucky times: horseback riding, skiing, walking barefoot along the ditch banks on little paths carved by the meanderings of my sister and me. We found a knotted-rope swing over the irrigation ditch in front of our house. From it we would fling ourselves from bank to bank and hang upside down, letting our hair trail in the water below. We would come home to my mother's complaints about the mud, the mess. How inconsiderate we were. Sometimes she would cry, just about the mud. And still, despite her tears and anger, we were lucky. We knew it.

When we went out to dinner my father would ask me to try new things: escargot, lobster bisque, steak in béarnaise sauce. What choices there were in the world, and how it impressed him when I learned to order on my own, in a perfect French accent like his.

Now I order for him. I try to get him to try different things on the menu at Denny's.

"How about an omelette, Daddy?"

"A what?"

"An omelette. Eggs."

"Oh no, no," he says. "Those are too complicated."

"Then how about meat loaf?"

"Meat what?"

"Loaf! Like Mommy makes."

"I never liked that." He frowns.

He orders the same thing every time. He wants a steak, with french fries. He wants a glass of water. Dessert, like an omelette, is "too complicated."

I am surprised how much I want, even yearn, for him to order omelettes and meat loaf, a French dip sandwich, grilled cheese, spareribs, salad, apple pie. Sometimes I argue with him about it. "You'll love it! You do love it," I insist. "No, no," he says. And "not right now," as if tomorrow or the next day he will change back into a gourmand, an eclecticist.

Why do I care? Why do I beg him, so shamelessly, to try things? People glance at us. I am being too pushy.

Is it because he once derived so much pleasure ordering for me? Or is it what I suspect, that I am trying to give him back all the food he loves, stop the floodwaters of memory from leaking out all the flavors and smells of his life? I want to teach him back himself, because a self seems too terrible a thing to lose.

Nothing, I am sure, is as evocative as a smell or a taste. For me, the scent of Mr. Clean switches on the projector to Jefferson Middle School, where they must have swabbed the floors every morning with the stuff. One whiff and I am there, in patchy low-riding jeans and hiking boots. I smell it and get worried about geometry.

And flavors. The taste of lemon meringue, a cloud on my tongue, whirls me back to the diner on Fourth Street in Albuquerque, sipping coffee with Daddy. He lights a cigarette—a Pall Mall—tilts his head back, and blows out the smoke. I let the meringue melt in my mouth; the lemon is sharp.

Food should ignite Daddy's memories, too, rein them back, bring him home. Brisket, quite simply, *is* my mother. Omelettes.

Pancakes. Pot roast. Strawberry cheesecake. Crêpes Suzette. Blintzes. If I can just preserve for him, say, hot fudge sundaes, I will have accomplished something in life.

I suppose I am simply trying, any way I can, to restore us to the other time, our lives, our happiness and even our unhappiness. If we act like before, do the same things, eat the same foods, maybe he will stop turning away from us. Maybe he will come back and life can begin to correct itself. Maybe he will remember.

I do it for Ava, too. Only on the other end. I consciously do things to create memories. I sing her the alphabet song. I talk to her in Spanish. I offer her a skinned cherry, cut in quarters. I feed her the pieces and say "I love you" each time she takes one. Maybe someday, in some future somewhere, my daughter will associate cherries with love.

Here is another memory: New York City, 1990. It is my graduation from Columbia University's MFA program, and the whole family is there. My parents have come all the way from New Mexico for the occasion. My sister has come from New Jersey. Daddy looks dapper; he has put on his favorite tie, which happens to be one I gave him in high school. It is wide and striped and terribly dated, but it fills me with emotion. We pose for pictures in front of the school's big gates.

"Everyone say cheese, everybody smile," says the passerby who agrees to photograph us. And there we stand, in the photograph, smiling, happy. Cheese.

There is Daddy, gap-toothed, wearing the striped tie. He stands beside my mother. She has a hand firmly affixed to his shoulder, gripped there as though it is important, as though he might walk away if she let go. There is something about him even then. Separate. Distant. Out of focus. He smiles but he does not look at the camera, rather at a place beyond it.

I remember my mother hugging me after the commencement and then turning to him: "Hug her," she said.

And then my father, turning toward her. "Who?" he asked.

It is just a moment. A small moment in an otherwise perfect, lucky day. But it gives me a start. A frisson that raises goose bumps on my arms despite the heat and sweat under the heavy blue gown.

To this day whenever I look at that picture of us, smiling and smiling, framed so perfectly by the spokes of the gates, I can hear his voice, small and strange, asking my mother who to embrace.

Now my mother is without him, in New Mexico. My husband is somewhere there, too, doing who knows what. And my father is here but not here. I constantly feel like I should clamp a hand on his shoulder, like my mother in the photograph, to keep him from floating away.

chapter 7

Repeating Dreams

Here is what I have learned: Shane made it to Gallup before the first snows, and from what I have heard from the three people I know there, just in time for the Jeep to break down. But it wasn't until now, with the arrival of the first really big snow here, that his absence has hit home. It occurs to me as the drifts begin to mount around the house that I am alone atop a mountain with two rambunctious dalmatian puppies, three cats, an old man, and a baby, in a big leaky, creaky house that heats with oil and wood.

I am not so great at chopping wood. First order of business: I must get better. Yesterday I used a jigsaw to cut pieces small enough for kindling for the woodstove—it was the only saw I could find. There are so many tasks labeled "male" in our lives that I never bothered with. For that, I now see, I shall dearly pay.

Second order of business, and one I do not relish: After chopping the wood and stacking smaller pieces as best I can, I put everyone in the car to return the female puppy, Franny. Two big dogs is one too many now, and Franny has a habit of jumping up on Daddy, each time nearly knocking him over. With Ava and me crying, Samo howling in the back of the car, and Daddy looking sort of stunned, we watch the Schumachers, the people who sold us the puppies, walk away with my darling Franny on a leash in front of their old house on Tunnel Road. Franny looks back at me once with an expression that seems to say "See ya."

Daddy approves: "That one is too jumpy."

Samo howls all night long, a terrible, longing howl that seems to express all our feelings. Daddy tells me that he misses my mother. Although I do not want to, I have to admit I miss Shane. Little things I never appreciated fully, the wrap and tangle of us in the mornings. Evenings, tearing lettuce for salad.

Ava misses him, too. For a week after he left she walked from room to room and even checked closets, peering in each doorway and saying "Da-da? Da-da?"

She does it less often these days. Only now and then do I see her peering into rooms and whispering "Da?" as if all this time he might have been just around a corner.

The house is filled with this music of missing, Samo and Ava's anthem to our loneliness.

In the mornings, Daddy has begun to get angry. Sometimes he throws things and bangs doors. "What the hell is going on around here?" he demands. He stamps his feet. He is so thin, he easily gets cold.

I wrap scarves around his neck and leave a hat on him indoors, which helps. And I have developed other strategies to calm him, too. Hot coffee and rye toast work okay but must be delivered immediately, before he gets too lost in his frustration.

His anger, like Ava's tantrums—which mostly have to do with teething—has a way of escalating if it is not quickly diverted.

When Ava starts to cry, I offer warm bottles of milk and favorite toys—singing Barney and talking Po the Teletubbie. I can even calm her down with a certain big red ball.

"Bawwl!" she says, smiling through her tears. She can't help it. The red plastic is irresistible; she tries to put her new front teeth on it, and then she tosses it across the room and chases it.

Daddy is harder. Sometimes I just sit and talk to him, answering the same questions over and over: "Now, precisely where is the location of this place? How did we get here? Who owns it? Where is my mother?"

Other times I read to them—Ava's books, which they both seem to enjoy.

"One fish, two fish," I say. They both smile. Daddy finishes: "Red fish, blue fish."

Other times I read him poems. When I was little he read me poems from *A Shropshire Lad,* a book he gave me. Now I put Ava on the rug with a bunch of toys, sit him down, and say, "Listen."

He likes the early poems of Allen Ginsberg, the work of Anne Sexton and Seamus Heaney. Perhaps he recognizes some of it. I read to him aloud, while he eats rye toast. I read him a poem by the Greek poet Yannis Ritsos called "The Statues," written in 1953:

> *He turned the key in the door*
> *To enter his house, to lie down.*
> *Suddenly he remembered that he had forgotten something.*
> *It was late, he couldn't go back.*

So, alone in the night,
With his hand on the key,
Away from the street, away from his door,
The whole man, facing his fate,
Turned into marble like the statues.

Yet the statues smiled indifferently.

When I stop reading and look up, I see the poem has made him cry. It is shocking to me—in my life I have only seen my father cry once, when his brother, my Uncle Sol, died. He has never been one to exhibit emotions of any kind. In fact, he always gave me the impression that he believed emotions were a sort of lesser form of mental activity, somewhere far below other, more analytical thoughts. That was why he rarely hugged and never really kissed us. He thought sentimentality was best left for old movies and dancing to Sinatra with my mom on our back terrace, after they thought we were asleep. Sometimes he would get choked up when he'd hear certain songs—like "Sunrise, Sunset" from *Fiddler on the Roof*. But never to the point of tears.

It is very disconcerting seeing him cry, and even he seems surprised. He wipes his face: "Water is coming down here." He points to the streaks in the corners of his eyes.

I hand him a tissue.

I decide that from now on I will read him light verse and things without reference to fate, memory, tragedy, or people missing each other. I will read him things with rhymes.

His own speech is pared down now, skeletal, like he has become. And eloquent. He himself has begun to speak in poetry.

When Ava walks into a room he says: "Here's the one that fills the room with hurricanes."

There is undeniable beauty in the way he is losing language, the way he substitutes different words when he cannot find the ones he wants. He calls toast "the singed bread," and apples "the crackly, magnificent, sweet ones." Sometimes he calls me and Ava "the beautiful big one" and "the beautiful little one."

Ava, meanwhile, is creating her own relationship to language. Some days Daddy is "Da-da-pop-pop," and I am "Mommy-moo." She sings songs that weave in and out of recognizable words. "Loo-de-loo-de-loo," she sings to Lulu, the cat. "Loo-loo-de-loo."

Occasionally Daddy will pick up on her singsong creations, and the two perform a duet. Then they laugh together, or smile, with appreciation for their artistry.

Samo also calms Daddy down. In the absence of his sister and the presence of the new chill that keeps us indoors, the dog has bonded to him. Sometimes he now sleeps at the end of Daddy's bed, draping his heavy paws over my father's legs. The cats, too, gravitate to Daddy. Some mornings he is completely cloaked in animals and has to dig his way out to get up.

I think he is calmed by their presence. Often he reaches down to touch one, instinctively. Lulu, nicknamed "mean kitty" for her tendency to scratch and claw, is subdued by him, and actually jumps into his lap and purrs. He has always liked animals. We had a cat named Sneakers when we were growing up that would come only to him.

Daddy's nightly roamings have become more frantic. He opens and slams doors, he dumps out the trash on the floor. Sometimes I find him on his knees, sifting through the mess.

But I have found that, if I catch it in time, together we can quell his panic.

It is something he started, one night when he woke from a particularly vivid nightmare. I heard him shouting and rushed in, then sat on the edge of his bed as he told me his dream, which I now know is always the same.

While he was telling me, I saw how it calmed him. I saw how it was good for him. Now I, too, have begun sharing my dreams. Or rather my dream. For I have a single dream, over and over, as well.

Sometimes I go first. Mine is that I find out I have to go back to high school because it has been discovered that I never finished a certain math class. The day I get back is the final exam, but I am not prepared. I stare at the test, trying to guess the answers. If I fill in the blanks I have a better chance of passing than if I leave them empty, but I am completely guessing. If I fail, everyone at work will find out and I will lose my job and probably the house, too. I have a sick and desperate sense of foreboding. All these years I have just been faking it, and now I have been caught, a life imposter.

Before my father tells his dream he always drinks a glass of water, then clears his throat. It is a ritual.

His dream is that he never got out of the Army. It is World War II and he is in Leyte Gulf in the South Seas with nothing but K-rations to eat and a bad case of athlete's foot. He is in the artillery. He sees people die; one is a young Jewish boy from Cleveland Heights, near where Daddy grew up. "He was just shipped in the day before, and poof, like that, he was gone," Daddy says.

Daddy's dream has blurred with an actual memory. On another occasion he has told me the story about the young Jewish boy as a real part of his wartime experience. In the real story my father added: "The boy wrote a letter to his parents, a long letter. He read it to me one night. It had descriptions of everything, Guadalcanal, the trip over, the ocean, which he had never seen before." Daddy paused for dramatic effect.

"I often think about that letter, because he sent it out the day he was killed. Our letters took a long time to get to our families. It is certain that the boy's family received his letter after they received the notification of his death in combat. Imagine that," Daddy said. "Imagine that family reading that letter after they knew he had been killed. It must have seemed like he was talking to them from another world."

I shivered and glanced at him. The story seemed almost allegorical, code for what is happening here. I thought then that perhaps the other world to which he was referring was the same world he was traveling to now. The planet of the missing, the absent, the lost.

As his brain roams, Daddy's speeches come in the form of florid dispatches from faraway places. On the phone it makes my mother furious. For years she has not seen his illness, cannot acknowledge it. She thinks he is just being difficult to annoy her. And the disease itself is so fluid that she can ignore the peculiarities and focus on the moments of lucidity, although as the weeks pass, they seem to become increasingly rare.

I decide not to force issues. When Daddy executes a sudden time shift, when he asks me for his sister or mother or directions to his office, I just listen, nod, and act like I understand. It seems more respectful. Besides, the things he says, the places he goes in his mind are interesting. I get curious about what he'll say next, where he'll go. Like the afternoon the wind blew really hard and a naked lilac branch rapped on the dining room window. Daddy said we had to hurry up and get outside. The parade was starting. We wouldn't want to miss the band.

—•◦❈◦•—

As the weather grows colder we thicken, growing stiff with layers of sweaters and socks. We spend more and more time inside.

The cold seems to anger Daddy. The house seems too close. The ghosts of Mommy and Shane lurk; we are surrounded by their things. My husband's paintings, a few of my mother's dusty tchotchkes that have somehow ended up here, keep reminding us that they are not.

Now, a month later, I am beginning to adjust to the idea of Shane's absence. Our marriage seems to be receding into the history of my life. It seems like a chapter now, a short time consumed by the present in which Daddy, Ava, and I are now living.

Strange, how I defined myself so completely as a wife, an identity that, as the days go by, seems less and less significant. Strange, the way I have traded in that identity, quite simply and suddenly, and become another person, a person who takes care of other people.

Before Shane, I had been both a single woman and a member of various couples in Manhattan. Each one seems like a separate life to me now, or a book I read, complete between two hard covers and now finished and shelved in a place I cannot find. Along the way I was a waitress, an archivist for a television museum, a library administrator, an assistant editor, a news clerk, a fact checker, a contributing editor, and a journalist. Many of those lives have evaporated. In their place is this life, in this creaky old house on Beartown Road, where I work for a small-town paper and am the mother of a baby named Ava and the daughter of a man named Sanford.

When Ava cuts a tooth she screams, clutches her jaw, and then holds her hands out in front of her desperately, like she just touched something hot. When she hears music she stands up and twirls until she is so dizzy she collapses. She sees her shadow move when she moves and she laughs. A deep belly laugh. The shadow is a joke she gets.

My father gets it, too. They often laugh together. She has a plastic alligator with a mouth that opens. She likes to put her finger in its mouth and say "Oh no!"

It cracks them up.

Then he puts his finger in the alligator's mouth. "Oh no!" he says.

She laughs so hard I worry that she will fall over or not get enough air and faint.

It has been a long time—twenty-four years—since I have lived with my father, since I have really felt like a daughter, and this time it is very different because I have a daughter, too. And my father has a granddaughter now. These are connections that, much of the time, escape him. My father does not always re-member who I am, so I have to tell him, "I am your daughter Beth, Daddy." Or, "It's me, Daddy, Beth, and this is your grand-daughter, Ava." I show him the pictures I have put about, family portraits of the four of us—my mother, sister, myself, and him, from long, long ago. "That is me, but who are these other peo-ple?" he asks.

Then I see it, but it is so hard to believe: We do not exist for him anymore.

The other lives that I have lived do not exist anymore, either, because there is nobody here who knows about them.

I do not hear from Shane. Few friends call. Those who do seem worried. I do not sound like my old self, they say.

They are right. I am not my old self. The things that were important to me, the way I have thought of myself, even the words I use to describe myself are shifting. It is becoming difficult to look back.

Like my father and my daughter, I am changing.

chapter 8

The Evaluation

e left you?" My mother is incredulous. "Bastard!"

"Shit," my sister says.

It is a conference call. My sister works for a telecomunications company; she is into complex communication arrangements. Often when I am speaking to her, she puts me on speakerphone or stops me midsentence and says, "Wait, I'll conference in Mom. Tell her that."

I tried to hide Shane's departure as long as I could. It was embarrassing. And why should I worry them? I asked myself. Maybe he would come back. Maybe everything would resolve itself.

That is beginning to seem unlikely. My mother hadn't anticipated this situation when they sent Daddy here, and I can tell she is wondering if it was the right thing to do.

"Shane was under a lot of stress," I tell them. "I was very angry about housework and stuff."

"You are too nice," my sister says.

"He deserves to be clonked on the head," says my mother. I

decide not to tell them right then about the other person, the one whose e-mails I have surreptitiously read.

They say never to read the diary of your lover. The modern version of that is, don't read his e-mail. This is true even if you haven't heard from him in weeks, and he is the father of your child. Don't do it.

Shane has seven e-mails from someone named Marty, all of them signed "with love." They are lusty notes that revealed to me that stress, Daddy, and my anger were not the only motivating forces in his move back West. I read them over and over, somehow addicted to the winces of pain certain sentences elicit. It gives me an interesting sensation. I feel my pulse rise, I feel overheated. I actually get large red blotches on my neck and upper chest.

I consider the possibilities. Maybe Marty is a man; maybe Shane is gay. I could be understanding about this. He didn't know how to break it to me. Although he certainly feigned it well in our marriage, maybe he just can't relate to the female physique.

I make a spate of phone calls to Gallup, to glean what I can. I call people I hardly know, just because they know him. But they don't say much. They've seen him around, but I can tell they don't want to get involved.

In addition to outright exhaustion from work and taking care of the animals, house, Daddy, and Ava, I now feel an enormous sense of victimhood. I carry it around all the time. It seems useful. A badge of pain. I have begun to imagine ways it can come in handy. I could take days off work just to play with Ava, like those happy-looking, stay-at-home moms I see in the grocery store wearing sweatpants and T-shirts in the middle of the week. I could spend time with Daddy. I've been left by my husband, after all.

I handle Shane's apparent affair in the finest tradition of American womanhood—I go get a haircut. And then I buy a car.

The haircut is blunt, shoulder-length, and I feel like someone different without the curls down my back that he admired. I am not hurt, I tell myself. I am a different woman. I have blunt hair. I drive a mauve SUV. He might not even recognize me.

A more important and complex task has been getting Ava into full-time day care on the days that Shane used to watch her while I worked. The people at Christ the King Day Care, a few blocks from my work, seem to like me. They read my articles in the local paper. I often write about child care and children. Being a minor celebrity can come in handy—they open a full-time spot for her.

But Daddy is home alone all day, wandering around the house, going in and out the front door. Smoking. I find the butts smashed out on the front porch. And then I find one inside, on the floor of the bathroom. In desperation, I ask the neighbors from across the road—Mr. and Mrs. Wright, an elderly couple who are retired farmers—to look in on him. Sensing something amiss, they have in the past, on their own, stopped by. From time to time they've even brought him food. Once they sat with him for an hour when he seemed particularly confused. He'd been in the front yard, sort of yelling at passing cars.

"The most amazing thing happened," he told me later. "These sweet people dropped in on me and brought me a nice meal. I think they were missionaries. Of course I completely skirted the topic of religion."

My father does not believe in God and enjoys pronouncing it. Over the years, my parents, atheists, got great shock mileage out of telling devout people that God did not exist. My mother spared nobody, not even our elderly Catholic cleaning ladies.

Daddy is holding on to this, even now, as his mind lets go of so many things. In the crumbling neurological structure of his brain, the nonexistence of God is a single thought, or antithought, that will not be erased. He brings it up now over dinner. Or in the car, apropos of nothing. Curious, how he remembers so well something he does not believe.

Not believing in any religion although simultaneously feeling very Jewish was a central complicating irony in my father's life. It was a leitmotif of many a family dinner conversation. It seemed like a complicated math problem Daddy was ever trying to work out. He believed it to be the height of human arrogance to construct a creator in man's image. An überman, with a judging capacity. But whenever someone suggested anything remotely anti-Semitic, he would instantly reclaim his Jewish identity. Once he said to me, "Being Jewish was never that important to me unless people hated Jews."

>———‹◊◊⚭◊◊›———‹

I so wanted things to be okay. I ignored the ways they weren't. It was a matter of personal pride, making things be okay. But it has become very clear: Our lives aren't working. When I come home in the afternoon, Daddy is in bed in his pajamas, the house is buried in papers. Things are moved all around. I can't find pots, pans, or hairbrushes. Cigarette butts litter the floor of the kitchen, the living room, the stairwell. "Why did you move all my bills?" I ask him. I am getting frustrated and tired. I want him to stop getting into things.

"I was looking for something."

"What?" I demand.

I figured it was his wallet or glasses, which get lost about once a day. The wallet contains four items: his driver's license; a studio portrait of him and my mother smiling dreamily, circa 1980; a picture of me when I was seven; and a slip of paper that says, *Sanford Cohen, age 80,* and an address and phone number for their house in Albuquerque. It is written in my mother's shaky handwriting and torn in several places.

His glasses are thick brown plastic and old. On one side is the sticky residue of some tape from a time an arm came off, before my mother took them to get fixed. They are the sort of glasses you can buy at pharmacies, but this pair is important because they work just right for him. He uses them for reading. It would be hard now to replace them, if they really became lost. Often I find him wearing them, by a lamp, bent over and studiously examining the contents of the wallet.

When he can't find his wallet or glasses he spends hours looking, and I used to help, thinking how awful it would be if they were lost, until I realized that he needs to look for them. Finding them brings him great satisfaction, a sense of accomplishment. I don't want to rob him of the experience. I try to sympathize with the act of searching.

But when I asked him today what he was looking for in the house he has decimated in chaos, he told me that it wasn't his glasses or wallet. He looked at me thoughtfully, considering, and said, "Let's see, I was looking for something all day, what was it? Hmmm. Not my glasses. Oh, I remember."

"What was it?" I demanded, looking around at the tumultuous house.

"Clues," he said.

———————⟨∞‖∞⟩———————

I need help.

I call my sister in Albuquerque, who tells me about the pain in her wrists. She has carpal tunnel syndrome. "My hands are going numb," she says. "I might have to get an operation."

I do not tell her about giving back Franny or about how Daddy cries sometimes. I don't tell her about how bad the laundry has gotten or how the unpaid bills are mounting on my desk simply because there is never time to attack them. But she senses.

"What are you going to do?" she asks me.

"I don't know, just keep doing what I am doing, I guess."

"If you ask me, you are in deep shit," my sister says.

"Thanks."

She says she'll send me a check. I am not sure what a check will do but I say okay, thinking it couldn't hurt.

I call my friends. Some of them have had parents divorce, break hips, turn mean, or die. My friends are pleasant, even nice, but in terms of actual real-world advice, they just shrug. None of them have ever been in my precise situation, taking care of their child and father simultaneously. They seem more interested in the disappearance of Shane than the decline of Daddy. I realize that I have become the subject of a chain of gossip among the people I know in New York City. People enjoy hearing about other people's misfortune. There is something satisfying about it. It puts their own problems in perspective.

I call the Alzheimer's Association. I tell them about Daddy and me and Ava, alone here on Beartown Road. I ask them, Are there any programs available that could help us? Is there any kind of assistance I could apply for? They tell me that there are all sorts of things out there, but we have to be formally evaluated. They tell me to contact the Office for the Aging, who, in turn, tell me they will arrange to send a team of social workers to our house.

A social worker and a nurse—two middle-aged women with matching short gray hair—arrive on a chill afternoon and knock on our door. Daddy, looking very dapper in a white cotton shirt fresh from a plastic package and a red sweater pullover vest, answers and invites them in. When I come downstairs the three of them are already seated in the living room, chatting away like old friends. The social worker introduces herself as Raya Schuter and her companion is introduced to me as "Nurse Johnson." They are a team, she explains, who go to people's homes to perform evaluations. Daddy looks interested and a bit embarrassed. "Evaluate?" he says. "Well, I don't know that there is anything much to evaluate, but I am certainly pleased to meet you."

He offers them something to drink. I notice that he is acting abnormally normal and I find myself wishing that he were still wearing the inside-out sweater he had on yesterday, his pants stained with urine.

The pair ask Daddy and me questions. Name, profession, age, and so forth. He answers ceremoniously, curtly, and to the point. More important, he answers right. He even remembers the year he was born: 1920. "I guess I am really getting up there," he says.

I am getting really annoyed. What a time for him to have a

bout of lucidity. Whether we can get some help depends on him being pretty out of it, and he is showing no signs of dementia at all. The women ask me questions, too. How old am I? Where do I work? Am I married?

Forty is not exactly young to be a mom, one points out. Maybe I am feeling stressed out as a single mom, they both suggest. Having one's husband leave can be traumatic, the nurse says. I feel the urge to kick her.

Then they start in with the financial questions. Does Daddy have any savings? Yes, I say.

Any property?

A house in Albuquerque.

Estimated value?

About $140,000, I say.

The two women exchange knowing glances.

Is Daddy on Medicaid? they ask.

He has health insurance; I get out his cards. He is a retired professor. He is a veteran of World War II. He has Medicare.

Daddy sits on the couch, smiling.

The women tell me they represent a program called CASA— which stands for Community Alternative Systems Agency.

"We are a program to provide services mostly for people on Medicaid," one explains.

Veiled meaning: Daddy has too much money. I have a flash of understanding. I am beginning to get what people mean when they talk about the elderly "spending down" their money to qualify for aid.

The social workers stay and chat awhile longer, admiring Ava, who climbs on Daddy's lap and plants a big kiss on his cheek. We are the picture of happy, happy normalcy. I feel like crying.

"Listen," I tell Raya Schuter, when Daddy goes to the bathroom, which he somehow finds without instruction. "He is really much more out of it that he seems today."

She smiles politely, as though she has seen it all before. "I understand, I do, this is a lot to keep together here."

I tell her I am away all day and my baby is in day care, that Daddy is all alone.

Isn't there any kind of help available? Something, anything? I ask her about caregiver respite, something I heard about at work. Apparently there are people who will come to your house for a few hours on a Saturday to give you a break to shop or see a movie if you are the caretaker of a person with Alzheimer's disease.

"That program is very popular, it has a long waiting list," she says.

Veiled meaning: Forget about it.

The social workers tell me that maybe I should contact the next county over, since we live in the country, so far away from their headquarters. "Try calling the Chenango County Office for the Aging, honey," the nurse suggests. They stand up to leave, and Daddy—with great chivalry—escorts them to the door.

"Nice visiting with you," he says. "Have a nice afternoon."

As they drive away he turns to me. "Such nice ladies," he says. "Are they our cousins?"

As the two women drive down Beartown Road and out of our lives, I feel like those people in movies who are stranded in the wilderness, waving their arms when a plane passes overhead.

We have lost our flares. The opportunity to be rescued has passed.

• • •

A few days later I get a report in the mail. Daddy is "independent with ambulation, bathing, dressing, and toiletry," it says. He has a "normal range of motion" and can feed himself. He may need assistance with shopping, transportation, and meal preparation, and with his finances as well as operating a telephone. "Daughter manages medication, laundry, and home."

The social workers send me pamphlets for various nursing homes and a home health care directory. They recommend that Daddy attend adult day care sponsored by a program called GROW.

When I call a few people in the directory they sent me, I learn their fees—they make as much as I earn as a journalist. "You should consider selling his house," someone suggests, "to free up some capital."

I try to imagine selling my parents' house. It would necessitate leaving work, getting on planes, traveling with Daddy and the baby, and then the whole deal with real estate people. I would have to talk to tax accountants and bankers. I would have to do at least a little math, a discipline in which I have no natural talent. I feel dizzy just thinking about it.

I wish the social workers could have just seen Daddy the morning I got their report. His face was shaved in some places and patchy with beard in others; he had a thin shaving cut across one cheek. He was wearing his underwear over his pants, an arrangement that served to emphasize how thin he has become. Normally his pants hang off him loosely. With the tight men's briefs on top you can see he is tiny as a teenage boy. He came in my room and woke me at 5:30 A.M. "Something is wrong here," he said.

"I'll help you, Daddy, just let me get up. I'll get that on you right."

The baby sat up and howled. Her diaper had come off during the night and she had slept all night on sheets soaked with pee.

"Oh good," he said. "I'll wait right out here."

He closed the door to the bedroom and stood right outside. I could hear him breathing out there, waiting for me.

chapter 9

The Blue Dot

—◦◦ ⋈ ◦◦—

Marty, it turns out, isn't a man. She is a girl. About eighteen. Yesterday, the day I found this out from one of Shane's friends, my father told me quite clearly he wanted to leave our house, go back to his mother. His mother, I tell him, has been dead for over forty years,

"You know what I mean," he says.

I do. He means my mother, his wife. Julia.

On the phone, my mother says she wants to try to be nicer. She talks to Daddy and tells him this. But she soon reveals she still hasn't accepted it, the disease that is eating his brain.

"There is no proof," she says to me. "He's just bored, he doesn't pay attention. He isn't interested in things."

"Mom, I am not going to argue with you about it."

"He should be here, with me," my mother says.

I have rarely understood my mother, or shared her sentiments in life, but at that moment I feel our circumstances push us together. We are connected by a thick cord of loneliness. I understand how she feels, wanting a husband back.

The family discusses it, and several phone calls later we decide to send Daddy back to Albuquerque, to Mommy. We all agree, they should be together. And I have another reason. My own private one that I do not share. The Alzheimer's Association has cautioned me: Leaving someone with Alzheimer's alone all day is dangerous. Daddy smokes constantly. He could start a fire. At least in Albuquerque, my mother is there with him during the day.

"He could wander, anything could happen," a woman named Donna Gavula told me. "You really should start thinking about alternative care."

That, I have now learned, is a popular euphemism. It means "nursing home."

Donna Gavula is an "aging services coordinator" at the Broome County Office for the Aging. She is really nice and makes me feel the way I do when I get a great waitress at a diner who calls me "honey" and keeps checking to see if my coffee is full. Donna calls me at home a few times, to check in. She tells me stories about happy families who have looked into alternative care. "Your father doesn't know what he wants anymore, you can't judge his happiness," she says. Then, she ventures: "He was never really a very happy person, was he?"

"I guess not," I say. Come to think of it, I don't remember my father ever whooping for joy, getting excited, or saying "I am so happy" about anything. He had those existentialist leanings that so many intellectuals have, which on a bad day can veer toward nihilism.

Because of this Donna says I shouldn't feel bad about "putting him someplace." Maybe that is the solution. Maybe I should look into it and broach the topic with my mother. Once he gets home and she realizes afresh how mixed up he is, she may regret sending for him.

I asked Daddy about it. How would he like to go and look at a few nursing homes? I tell him about Donna, how she told me how content the elder people were, once they got settled.

"They have activities," I tell him. "They have checkers."

"See this?" he said, pointing to his temple with his index finger, cocked like a pistol. "That is where I want to stick a bullet if it comes to that."

In the morning it happens. I smell it from upstairs. A smell that sets off all the bells and whistles. I take the stairs by threes. Daddy has accidentally lit a small fire in the wastebasket in the bathroom. When I walk in it is already out; he has poured water on it with the toothbrush cup. He is waving away tiny clouds of smoke and coughing. "Got this goddamn mess in here—a sort of collusion of paper and flames occurred in this receptacle thing."

"Oh God, Daddy. People warned me about this."

"What sort of people?"

"Just people," I say.

I don't want to be angry. I don't want Donna Gavula to be right about Daddy. I decide not to tell her about the fire, but I have to admit, it shakes me up like nothing before in my life. I am beginning to see her point about danger.

The night before Daddy is to return to Albuquerque, he and Ava and I drive to Syracuse and get a motel room. He will fly out in the morning and change planes once, in Oklahoma. The airlines have a special program for dementia patients. He is to wear a name tag with a blue dot on it. All night long he keeps asking me if I have the name tag ready, if the blue dot is on it. I let him see it over and over, and finally he falls asleep clutching the tag in his right hand.

At three in the morning I sneak away and take a bath. It is a secret pleasure, soaking in solitude in the clean porcelain motel tub with its perfect bar of wrapped Ivory soap and bleached-white washcloth. When I come out, Daddy has the light on and has unpacked his suitcase. Some of his clothes are on top of Ava, burying her. I pull them off.

"Where in the hell are we?" he says angrily. "Where is my wallet?"

"We are in Syracuse, Daddy. You are flying home to Mommy in about three hours. Everything is all right."

"It will never work. This is a meshuggeneh plan, I will get lost somewhere in the Midwest."

"Daddy, you have to believe me, they have a special program for you. You just have to wear this name tag and they will escort you."

He sees the name tag. He picks it up. "This blue dot, this tells them?"

"Yes, Daddy. The blue dot."

"Why blue?" he asks.

I tell him I do not know.

In the morning we drive from the motel to the airport in the snow. Even though it is mid-November, a few businesses along the way have already put up Christmas decorations, plastic snowmen, lights, and mechanical Santas who wave at us and say "Ho, ho, ho" and "Merry Christmas!" which makes Ava shriek with laughter. The road is icy. The windshield steams up. Daddy asks me over and over where he is changing planes, where he is going. I get off at the wrong exit. We drive down empty streets, looking for signs to get back to the highway. I stop at a gas station and ask directions. Daddy is very nervous. He thinks he will miss his plane, even though it is hours until it departs.

Everything feels wrong. The roads and signs seem all mixed up. The seat of the car is slightly wet from where I spilled my cup of bad motel coffee. I am beginning to question the very idea of the whole plan. Daddy and Ava and I are doing okay, we are getting by. What would it be like for him to suddenly find himself in a different place yet again? What if he did get lost in the Midwest, and the blue dot didn't work? Can Mommy handle Daddy, who seems more confused every day? And what will it be like when he is gone?

I will miss him, I realize. The feeling settles over me darkly. Ava and I will be alone.

Finally I get proper directions to the airport. I have gone in the opposite direction, and we drive through neighborhoods and down streets lined with gas stations and stores. While we're driving we listen to the radio: Billie Holiday, Nat King Cole, "Greensleeves." Daddy always sings along, even though the voices get fuzzy with static. The music makes him forget to be worried. "The bells are ringing," he sings, emphatically, "for me and my gal!"

There is something about him that operates just like those radio stations. Sometimes he is tuned in, clear, alert; other times he becomes obstructed by static. In and out he tunes, searching for a station in his mind. He slips into static now.

"I just have one question," he says. "Where exactly are we and where are we going?"

In the airport we buy doughnuts, orange juice, and coffee and sit in leather seats, waiting. We are there two hours early. Ava crawls, then pulls herself up and toddles quickly down the tiled corridor and back, over and over. We take turns chasing her. She likes to go really fast and then slide on her diapered bottom along the shiny, newly waxed floors. Before I can stop her, she crumbles a doughnut into tiny pieces and then jumps on them, grinding crumbs into the carpet in the waiting area. She pulls the last piece of doughnut from my hand and tosses it across the aisle of seats, then runs laughing after it. She watches me on my knees, trying to sweep the crumbs into a napkin.

She loves the power of defiance. She is triumphant. "Jump!" she says.

Then she sees a man. He has disheveled blond hair and a black leather jacket. He has one leg crossed over the other the way Shane sometimes sits. He looks at his watch, opens a newspaper. Ava, momentarily sitting on my lap between bouts of doughnut dismemberment, escapes my arms and scoots across the waiting area to where the man sits. She throws her arms around his leg. "Da! Da!" she shouts. "Da!"

The man looks down uncomfortably at the toddler attached to his pant leg. Then he looks up to see who might be the responsible parties. I wave and head over to reclaim her. Ava clings with fury. "Mommy, Da!" she says.

My father turns to me. "Is that the baby's father?" he asks.

"No, Daddy, it isn't," I say, and for the first and last time since Shane left, hot tears stream in ribbons down my cheeks.

chapter 10

Staying On

———◦◦※◦◦———

Daddy made it back to Mommy in Albuquerque. He did not get lost in the Midwest. The blue dot worked.

For the last few days, things have been very calm. I am adapting to life alone with Ava and the animals. I am adapting to life without Shane and Daddy. It is still demanding. Up at 6:00 A.M., feed animals, put dog outside to run, let cats out. Bathe and diaper Ava. Dress and feed her. Dress self. Let dog back in.

Now Ava looks for Daddy all the time. She runs to his room in the morning and pushes the door open and looks dumbfounded by his absence. "Pop-pop?"

Strangely, my father's absence leaves an even larger hole in our lives than Shane's. Maybe this happens because now we are reduced to two. Two people in a big, cold house. Even without focus, without memory or the right words for things, Daddy was a presence and a comfort. Even though I had to answer his questions all the time.

Things go on.

I think: Daddy has the right idea. There is peace in forgetting, there is an elegance and grace to it. You focus on the present moment, let everything else fade away.

Thanksgiving veers toward us in a blizzard of advertisements. Ava brings home from day care a drawing of a turkey striped in blue Crayola. My mother calls and tells me that she and my father will be going to Seattle, moving in with my sister, who relocated. They will have Thanksgiving there. It was too hard, she says, alone with Daddy in Albuquerque. She can't do it, can't take care of him alone. "I understand, Mommy," I say.

I have made a decision. It feels good to do so, almost like taking a political stand. I have decided that Ava and I will skip Thanksgiving. I do not feel particularly thankful, so there seems no point. I think that all that food—turkey, cranberry sauce, stuffing—would be lost on Ava.

But out of the blue, an invitation arrives from across the road. The elderly farmers, Gene and Betty Wright, ask us on Thanksgiving morning to come over and have a midday meal with their children and grandchildren. So much for my grand justifications, ranging from compassion for the downfall of native people to disdain for commercialism.

We get there the same time as the Wrights' son, Mark, his wife, Janet, and their five children, four matching little girls (three with blue eyes, the youngest with brown) and a blue-eyed baby boy, Marky.

The Wrights' house fills with the medley of children, playing and laughing. Danielle, the eldest girl, and Courtney, the youngest, play with Ava. They are showing her how to slide off the side of the couch and hit the soft carpet. "Boom, boom," Ava mimics.

She is in heaven. It was the right thing, coming over. It has been awful at home, with Ava asking every few minutes this morning for Da and Pop-pop.

Over dinner Betty casually asks me how my father is doing. "I sent him back to Seattle to be with my mom," I say. "They missed each other."

Everyone nods, approvingly. A married couple should be together, even if they are sick.

Nobody brings up Shane.

It hasn't been that long since he left, but already he seems like a stock character in a movie, the one played by a sensitive actor like William Hurt. The character who means well but just can't do the right thing by the people he loves.

When Daddy was with us, I was too busy to be angry, too busy to even address the sense of betrayal I feel. It seemed to me that the instant he boarded the plane, my pain swelled. Thoughts began to tumble into my mind, anger and hurt competed for my brain time.

Driving back from Syracuse had been hard. I'd had a sudden urge to go the wrong way, toward Watertown, toward Buffalo, toward Canada. Simply leave the life Shane and I had created. After all, he had. I, too, could start fresh. But there were the animals, Samo and the cats. There was my job at the paper.

For a moment, at the turnoff to I-81, I had paused. But then it had passed. I had driven the way we had come, to Beartown Road, for better or worse.

Ever since the day we moved into our farmhouse, the Wrights have been friendly. Back in the summer, on humid afternoons, they invited us to swim in their pool. Ava loved it; she'd toot around in an inflatable plastic car, pulled by their granddaughters, laughing joyfully.

The entire family came to Ava's first birthday party in October. They brought her a stuffed dog from the television show *Blue's Clues*. She fed it her bottle, the highest compliment. When Mr. Wright mowed his lawn, he sometimes would slip across the street and mow ours, too.

Earlier in autumn, their son, Mark, took Ava and me on a hayride with his daughters, on a cart attached to their big tractor, all over their farm. I got a feeling then for the enormity of their property—we went by the numerous ponds and woods and through bumpy fields that made Ava, who was holding hands with Courtney, screech with pleasure. She kept saying "Bump bump."

I hadn't thought much about it, these neighborly gestures, but now suddenly, set against the relief of our situation, they seem more important. Their humanity, heaven-sent. From time to time, for example, the couple has begun to bring us plates of food.

They are not without their own troubles. Betty looks very tired, and I have noticed a distinct tremor in the right hand of Mr. Wright. Still, it is clear that he is an enormously capable man very much in control of his life. Probably in his seventies, he meticulously grooms his property and in the summers skims clean the surface of the pool every day. When we first moved in, he told me the story of his old barn.

"It burned down, and I figure I know who did it," he said. "A troop of Boy Scouts were hanging around here that day. Never knew for sure, but it had to be. Probably playing with matches."

I had heard from another neighbor that all his animals, cows and horses, were still inside when it went up in flames.

Mr. Wright is quiet, with playful, sparkling eyes that have a hint of sadness in them, perhaps from the night he heard the screams of his livestock, perishing in the inferno inside the old barn. He said that was it for him. He would never keep animals again.

He and his wife are simple people, good people, people who have worked hard and reaped the rewards, a nice home with a view of a pond, a comfortable retirement. And now, as winter creeps toward us, their proximity, once a detail on the horizon of my life, feels important, like knowing you have an extra blanket in the closet. Not just because Mr. Wright is the sort of man who comes over with an oil lamp when the power is down, but because, like the bears I imagine living in the woods off Beartown Road, they are a presence rather than a void. And although I sense they are very much aware that things are not going well here in our home, still they somehow respect me. Once Mr. Wright told me he could tell that I am a strong woman. It is a word I would never have used to describe myself.

At Thanksgiving we talk about the food we are eating, we talk about recipes, we talk about Janet Wright's efforts to home-school her kids.

The turkey is good. Ava eats some, and three helpings of stuffing. Janet tells me all about the culinary leanings of her children and then asks me what Ava usually eats. "What's her favorite food?" she inquires.

I balk. A blank opens in my mind in relation to her question. Uh-oh. Do babies have favorite foods? It dawns on me that

I haven't been paying enough attention to Ava. I haven't been focusing on her habits or her tastes at all.

In fact, all my baby development books have been un-opened for weeks; the parenting magazines I subscribe to lie stacked by the front door with all the other unopened mail. They belong to the past now, when I was a person involved in such things. Since Daddy came and then left, and since Shane left, I seem to have dropped out of motherhood, at least the motherhood I used to know. Now the whole project seems changed. I am always tired, but not too tired to be consumed with worry. I lie beside Ava at night, watching her eyelashes flutter, placing my hand on her forehead. I fear that something, anything, will happen to her, to this perfect creature. The only remaining person in my life.

I hadn't really noticed, until the moment Janet asks me what Ava likes to eat, how much I'd changed. This woman serving me turkey is homeschooling, and I don't even sterilize Ava's bottles anymore. Or, for that matter, open my mail.

Her children are obedient, too. They sit on the couch in a row and take turns quietly playing with a toy. Ava, meanwhile, screeches when her turn is over and throws the toy rather than passes it on.

"Ava likes broccoli. She likes rice," I say to Janet Wright, trying to seem like I am on top of things. In truth, she had a handful of Cheerios minus the milk for breakfast.

"That's good!" Janet says. "A lot of kids won't eat anything but McDonald's these days."

Ava suddenly looks drawn and thin to me compared to Janet's kids. Marky is enormous, a great pumpkin of a child with rolls of muscley fat. I wonder what toll Ava has paid during these months. I can't help but think of all she should be getting from me, and isn't.

We have pie and ice cream and cookies for dessert, and then Ava and I take our leave. "Thank you so much," I say to Mr. Wright, who ceremoniously pats me on the back and gives Ava a big hug. He loves children; he pays special attention to Ava and, I now notice, always remembers her name. Betty hands me a plate of leftovers.

I realize as we depart that these people feel sorry for me. I am the subject of pity. "Will you stay on through the winter?" Betty asks me ominously, as if because my father and husband are gone I might pack up and leave.

"Of course I am staying on. Where would I go? I have my job. We have the dog."

As if a dog or job were reasons to stay on an old farm alone with a baby and winter coming on fast.

———— ◄◄••H••►► ————

I guess the Wrights knew what I didn't.

They know what the bears of Beartown Road must know—that winter, like life, can be really, really mean. Our first winter—the winter of 1998—had been abnormally mild. It had given a false impression.

I am learning the true definition of winter now. I am coming to respect it. Raised in Albuquerque, a place with average winters, where the snow always melts by afternoon, I have lacked a decent understanding of the season. And in New York City, you can ford streets, jump in cabs. Not so Port Crane, where, I have recently learned, winter typically runs from sometime in November up to May. A June snow is not unusual.

Furthermore, we live atop the second-highest hill in Broome County, a spot that once seemed grand and now seems ruthless, granting us special-delivery snowfalls that the lower elevations don't get.

It seems strange to me that Shane and I didn't consider such things as cold and snow when we bought this house. Back then, cold was just something that made life more cozy. An excuse to build an attractive fire. In 1998—the winter, people joked, "that wasn't"—we actually felt deprived of our fair allotment of cold.

Now, in December, as the days grow shorter, colder, and lonelier, and the snow gets deeper—in drifts I can no longer walk through—I often think of the bears snoring in their dens. Hibernation, when you think about it, is an excellent idea.

It is good the bears are all asleep now, because they can't see how slovenly I've gotten. I forgot to take the garbage out on two consecutive Thursday nights, and it heaps on the front porch.

The mailbox is full to overflowing. A few loose pieces of junk mail have made neat pockets in the new snow. The mailbox was blown off its stand in a recent storm. It lies on its side on the road, where I leave it, dented and abused, like roadkill. This does not discourage the mailman, who wipes clear a path to it and stuffs it even fuller each day with junk mail. I think maybe I am being punished for the crime of mailbox negligence. I seem to get every leaflet and sales promotion in the world.

Stores are selling imitation Christmas trees and fun winter wear. I pick up the wet circulars by the handful and stuff them into garbage bags. I can't stand the pictures of happy families opening presents. I turn away from the image of the smiling husband with the toddler on his shoulders, both wearing spanking-new down jackets that come in colors like Evergreen, Sky, and Mist. Junk mail assaults me with reminders of what I no longer have.

On colder days, when I go to work, I put Samo in Shane's art studio. Oh God, Shane would kill me. There are two parts of the studio, a big workshop and a smaller antechamber Shane used for an office. Unable to leave the dog outside in the howling winds and snowdrifts, I put the poor guy in the small office, where he goes wild, tearing up everything in sight. He has eaten several paintings in progress and has gotten into all Shane's stuff. I know it is wrong, but I take a perverse satisfaction in it. His stuff—which he just left behind—is getting trashed. There is a fairness to it, a symmetry to misfortune, no matter how harsh.

Yes, the bears would be ashamed of me. I have really let things go. And, apparently, acquired a mean streak. On occasion, passing Shane's studio, I have an urge to spit.

<hr />

Along with the snow and ice has come a woman named Alison Bert. A classical guitarist who is going through a midlife career change, she is interning at our paper and needs a place to stay. Partly for the company, partly for the little cash she pays us that helps with day care costs, I invite her here to room with us. She stays at our house Monday through Thursday, then goes back to Syracuse on the weekends, where she lives with her three pet rats.

During the week she sometimes eats with us and hangs out. She talks about the woes of life as a classical musician, the difficulty of touring, how hard it is to teach people with little talent and discipline.

She once met the great classical guitarist Andrés Segovia. I tell her how I once saw Segovia, too. He was judging a guitar contest at a church in Manhattan, and I just happened to wander in from the street. It was sort of a scandal, because Segovia decided nobody would win. Nobody was good enough.

Alison appreciates the story. I can tell she, too, thinks people don't make the grade. There is a deficit of excellence in the world. She freely shares her thoughts about our lives.

"I don't know how you can stand it here in the middle of nowhere!" She shakes her head. "It seems much too hard."

Another time she says, "I could never be a mother, I just don't have the nurturing instinct. I don't know how single mothers do it."

It is the first time I have actually thought about it: I am a single mother. It sucks my breath away.

I realize that everything is up to me. From here on out, I will change every diaper. I will wipe every tear. I will cherish every new word learned and celebrate every accomplishment in my daughter's life by myself. I will light her birthday candles and help her blow them out. I will help her with her homework, put Band-Aids on her knees. I alone will smell the beautiful scent of her breath at night, as sweet as lilacs.

But then I think, I *have* to do this, because there is no alternative. Because Ava is mine and I am hers, and we do not have the distraction of anyone else.

I suppose I am a statistic and that it is a stigma I must bear. I will walk around from now on as if emblazoned with a red letter S, for single mom. I suppose I will have to tell people—at work, on applications for things, on my taxes. I suppose I should start thinking about divorce. I suppose I will get used to this.

Interestingly, there is a part of me that is enjoying it. I

should be miserable: I have been left by my husband. But it is not all that bad. I have begun to notice that the life of a woman and her daughter can have a pleasant rhythm. I have a sense of delicious victimhood, "us against the world."

When Daddy was here we were pinch-hitting daily, we had no regular mealtimes, I did laundry when there was nothing to wear; we fell asleep when we could no longer stand being awake. We ate when our stomachs rumbled.

Now Ava and I are getting a system for nighttime. Eat, bath, book, bed. This is probably obvious to most families, but for me it is a revelation. Once, Shane and I had taken turns with stories and baths; now it is just me reading or putting bubbles on my chin to make Ava laugh. I can change a diaper with one hand. I am getting good at her. And we have a sweetness. She will walk over sometimes, for no reason at all, and say "Mommy kiss."

These are silent, private pleasures, not visible to the outside world. They are our secret rituals. Alison doesn't know or can't imagine how *hard* could translate to *challenging,* how a rotten deal can be invigorating somehow. How, set against the backdrop of all that has gone wrong, everything right seems heightened. She is awed by the hardship of our lives, the long drive from my job at the paper out to Beartown Road, bringing in the wood, starting the fire. What she doesn't see is how I am blinded by the glare of all the silver linings. Our sweet, lick-crazy dog. This child with great, mooning eyes. The view from the top of the road of a dozen hills, receding in shades of purple.

She could never do such hard work, or live in so remote a place, she assures me, although she does admit she likes the cats and could probably stand taking care of them (if it weren't for her rats). Especially Twy-twy, the tiny cat somebody dumped on our front porch last summer. Twy-twy sits on her lap and purrs in the evenings, redeeming us.

At my age, forty, Alison tells me over and over that neither motherhood nor the country is for her. There are too many exciting things she wants to do with her life. She needs to live in a city, with cafés and restaurants. She needs culture. She wants to work for *The New York Times* or the *Chicago Tribune* as a music or art critic.

She is thin with small lips, rather large front teeth, and short black hair. She wears short skirts with tights and nice sweaters and drives a new car. Her writing for the paper is considered peppy, one editor told me. During the week she worries intensely about the rats. "I hope they don't miss me too much," she says. "They aren't used to being alone." One of them isn't well, she confides. "Tumors."

Alison sits by the fire with me after Ava falls asleep and tells me that I should hate my husband.

"I hate him," she says, "and I haven't even met him."

She seems to feel it is her duty to constantly remind me how much my life sucks. Still, having her with us is pleasant, because she plays classical guitar music in her room for hours before we fall asleep: Villa-Lobos, Chopin, Brahms. She is very good.

For a couple weeks, she has been a presence in the house that doesn't fit the space left by the absences of Daddy and Shane, but there she is anyway. I see now how any person can be better than no person at all.

In spite of Alison's observations and reminders that I should hate my life, things really do seem to be all right. I tell myself so every day. It is much easier than when Daddy was here. I no longer have to worry about fires in wastebaskets or missing keys.

I have begun, on the weekends, to take Ava and Samo to Nathaniel Cole Park, a few miles from our house. We hike on the snowplowed trail a mile and a half around a lake. I point out the V's of migrating geese to Ava. She rides on my back in a purple backpack that Shane and I bought for a trip we took to Greece last spring. On that trip she was tiny and often fell asleep. Now she is heavier and squirms. She wants out. "Docha," she says. "Bikabbebedocha."

Possible translation: "Let baby out, this is boring, the dog is clearly having all the fun on this walk."

We walk on along in the silence of the snowy woods. Occasionally a cracking branch will startle us, or a clump of snow will cascade to the ground at our approach. We just keep moving. A family of two, surviving.

⸻

All my relationships must come to an end, it seems. Maybe it's the huge mess that appears to make and remake itself in the house, no matter how much I tidy. Or maybe Shane is right, it is the anger I carry, a package I cannot put down. Once, when he was still here, I came home and found both Daddy and Ava soaked to the skin in their own urine. "Jesus, Shane," I said. "Would it be too much trouble to give a damn?"

Another time, when he forgot to take out the garbage for the second week, and several bags, stinking to heaven, clogged the porch, I took one and emptied it on the kitchen floor. Eggshells and coffee grounds and cat litter mingled with spoiled cottage cheese and Kleenex. "Whoops," I said. "I spilled the garbage."

And walked away.

But it was Alison who got angry two nights ago, when I came home late and she was locked out and had to eat her Chinese takeout in her car. Her internship is ending, she said, and she will soon go back to Syracuse.

Beartown Road is too far away from the paper and I am too undependable, she says. For her remaining days of work she will stay at the Red Roof Inn. It makes me sad.

This morning she presented me with a fist-size plastic backpack with a miniature Ferbie in it for Ava and a bar of handmade soap for me. "I hope things work out for you," she said.

I told her I hope things work out for her, too. And the rats.

———◦◦❦◦◦———

For now, we make do.

In addition to the feeling of occasional contentedness that has begun to visit me, so does its partner, ennui. Something about the defection of Shane plus Daddy's leaving has made me not care. When Daddy was here, it seemed imperative to at least try to keep organized and on top of chores. Now it seems somehow pointless. It's like I am applying the philosophies of Camus to housekeeping. Messes come, messes go, we'll all be dead someday. It hardly matters.

I used to enjoy doing dishes and laundry. There was a nice feeling in having the house clean and things organized. Now I have lost all interest. I pick through great piles of dirty laundry for our clothes each morning, searching for the quasi-clean, the acceptable. Disgust rises in my throat, slightly bitter, but not enough to motivate.

I can feel it at Ava's day care, where people are staring. I look like crap, and Ava isn't dressed as cutely as the other babies.

Her shirts and pants never match. Her curly brown hair seems to attract things that are sticky. Many of the other children are still at the crib and swing stage, while Ava has long ago mastered the crawl and alternates between it and her lightning-fast toddle. By the end of each day this regimen has left her filthy. Some nights, I am too tired to bathe her. I clean her up with wipes.

A woman who works at the day care facility named Judy McDonald has taken an interest in us. She is raising her grandson, Chandler. She is very motherly. She tells me to call her Grandma Judy. "Everybody does," she says.

Grandma Judy takes Ava home with her after day care so I can work late on my articles. When I come to pick her up, Judy tells me to sit down and eat. She makes spaghetti and meatballs and I eat with her and her husband, Joe. I wash the food down with big glasses of Kool-Aid. It is so quiet sometimes during these meals you can hear everyone chewing.

Judy tells me everything will be okay. About five different men have left her alone with her kids, she took care of her mother with Alzheimer's, and she made it through. "If it doesn't kill you, it makes you stronger," she quips.

She has survived: She drives a brand-new green Toyota SUV and lives with Joe in a big old farmhouse on the Susquehanna River, with an aboveground pool in the backyard. She has the largest collection of Barbies I have ever seen—all still preserved in cellophane in their original boxes. Some of them are the same ones I had when I was a little girl. I remember their expressions and hairdos, their tiny sunglasses and spike-heeled shoes that slipped onto their permanently molded high-heel-ready feet. One has the very same green silk dress mine had. They must have manufactured millions of them. Another has the same black-and-white-striped strapless bathing suit. In Judy's house, the Barbies have a special shelf that wraps around the living room, up near the ceiling. They stare down at us, a permanent beauty pageant.

Joe says one of the disadvantages of living on the river is that when it warms up a little you can hear the cracking of the river ice, as big slabs separate and collide in the current. It is very loud. I can tell that he sort of likes it, though. It must be exciting. Maybe for him the buckling river ice has the same slightly scary yet pleasurable quality as the bears do for me. The bears remind me that there is another world out there besides the one we inhabit. There is a whole universe, with its own daily dramas that dwarf us like the exploding stars about which we ran a wire story in our paper. So what if it's cold, if the baby has an ear infection and you have been left by your husband? Galaxies are being sucked into oblivion. Animals are becoming extinct. Ice-bound rivers are cracking.

When Grandma Judy changes jobs—from Christ the King Day Care to Magic Years up the street, I move Ava, too. It isn't just loyalty, it's practical. Judy helps me a lot. She advises me to spend some time on my laundry and house. "Don't let things get too far gone, you'll feel better."

A couple of times Ava and I have even stayed over. We watch television together in their living room and Joe shows me his pet—he keeps a rat, too, in a big aquarium. It seems like an enormous coincidence—that I should meet the only two rat owners of my life within weeks of each other. Plus it gives me something to talk about with Joe. I tell him about Alison's rats, how one is sick. He nods sagely. "They get that way," he says.

Grandma Judy's guest room has a great, cushiony bed with

vintage Cabbage Patch dolls on it. She has positioned a television so that you can lie down and click through cable channels. We don't have cable at our house. Sleepless in their house on the river, with Ava dozing beside me, I watch reruns of *Baywatch* and then infomercials for machines that roast chickens and strengthen abdominal muscles on the Direct2U Network, which takes over a local channel around two-thirty. I try to decide which I need more—roasted meats or a stronger stomach. It seems like you need one to deal with the other.

At Grandma Judy's, while Ava snores I feast on a smorgasbord of old movies and on news from the Philippines and Africa. I watch C-SPAN and Court TV. Other people's lives have problems, too. With cable you do not have to watch so many infomercials. You can kiss off those people who will teach you how to make a fortune buying foreclosed real estate. Click.

I learn the cardinal rule of cable: If you click long enough, there are always reruns of *M*A*S*H* somewhere.

Samme, my colleague at the paper, and Grandma Judy each invite us to Christmas. I decide, in a moment of surreal optimism, to try to do both. Judy puts up all sorts of decorations in her house, tiny electric train sets, a whole Santa's village full of movable people and tiny houses with lights, and an electric Santa and Mrs. Santa on her mantel that wave and say "Ho, ho, ho" just like the electric Santas on the roofs of Syracuse.

On Christmas Eve morning we head first to Judy's. Ava plays with Chandler and Grandma Judy's new shi tzu puppy. She tries to grab the people off Judy's electric Santa's village. Chandler makes Ava pretend to cook with him in a plastic kitchen. Ava prefers Chandler's trucks; she makes a *brrrr* sound and moves them across the floor.

Judy has bought Ava clothes, pacifiers, bottles, socks, and toys, and a green Dipsy the Teletubbie with plastic blue eyes. Ava and I give Chandler a toy truck that pulls a trailer with a boat on it.

Ava loves Judy and Chandler, but she is starting to get cranky. Feeling her forehead, I can tell she is clammy and a little feverish.

After opening our presents, we head over to Samme's in Delaware County, where we plan to spend the night. It is a long drive, with Samo in the back of the car getting frisky. The roads are empty because it is Christmas. I get stopped by a trooper somewhere around Delhi who takes one look in the car and apparently feels bad for me, a woman alone with a baby on Christmas. I was apparently going eighty. He asks, "In a hurry?"

"We're trying to get to Christmas dinner and I just took my baby's temperature and it is a hundred and three." It probably isn't even a lie. Ava is frantic, screaming in the backseat. Samo pipes in with a howl. We are a pathetic group. The car is a mess.

"Hospital is up ahead at the third exit," the trooper tells us. "Hundred and three is pretty high. I have a baby myself that age," he confides. He points at his mouth, which is filled with chewing tobacco. "Teeth."

We get to Samme's at three in the afternoon. She, her husband, Brad, and her mother live in an old farmhouse they restored, with about eight cats, six geese, a handful of brown hens, and a dog. When we walk in, dinner is just about to begin. There is a medium-size gathering of nice people: a couple from Australia, a woman from South Africa, a man from Chicago, and several locals. Sometime during the evening there is a fracas in the yard. Samo has caught one of Samme's prized chickens. Brad goes out and frees it with the help of his brother. They fix up a small pen for Samo, out of the wind. Then they place a heat lamp usually used to warm baby chicks near the enclosure so he will be warm. It is an ingenious arrangement. How useful men can be, when they do not leave you.

One couple at the party has a little boy, about seven, who runs around and around the room like a windup toy. For a while this distracts Ava, who decides to try to follow him, but then she gets bored and cranky and starts whining. The whining soon evolves into a full-blown tantrum. I touch her forehead; her fever has spiked again. The pain of teeth pushing through gums has turned her wild, twisting and screeching, unlike the baby I know. She cannot be comforted. She whines for the next four hours and into the night. The whines turn into cries and the cries into screams, long, bloodcurdling shrieks that stiffen her whole torso. I walk her up and down the staircase for hours, rocking her in my arms, trying to settle her. Samme's mother, an elderly woman who has recently lost her husband and broken her hip, looks at me helplessly, as if she wishes there were something she could do. She is thoughtful and even holds Ava for a while, soothing her, until it becomes clear that there is no soothing to be done. Ava has fallen into an abyss of baby misery. Her sobs have reached that point where you wonder if she can get enough air in between them.

"It's okay. It's okay. Go to sleep Ava, go night-night." I rub her back. I sing to her our calm-down song: "Walking around, walking around, Ava and Mommy are walking around."

There is no calm to be had. Her mouth is on fire. She slaps her cheek and clutches her gums. The last drop of the Infants' Tylenol was gone hours ago, spilled on the bathroom floor. Stupidly, I had failed to replenish supplies earlier in the week. It is typical of me now. Once I was the mother who traveled with a neat bag full of baby accoutrements. I was übermom, ready for anything. Now I am always running for diapers and wipes in the middle of the night. I lost that bag a month ago, and now I haul her stuff around in a plastic sack.

Finally, around 4:30 A.M., Ava drops off in a sweat to a fitful slumber. I never do sleep, lying beside her instead, watching her writhe and dream of something awful that causes her forehead to crease.

In the morning we open presents—really nice presents—that seem to cheer her. She especially likes tearing off the paper.

Samme's mother has been collecting my articles from the paper for months and has fashioned a beautiful book for me in which they are neatly mounted. Ava gets pop-up books and a stuffed poodle. But we can't enjoy ourselves for long. Ava is whining, revving up again for a tantrum. She rips the flaps out of the pop-up book. Samme and Brad look on pityingly. "Merry Christmas," they say.

We head out on the road, where the full-throttle hollers begin. "Jingle bells, jingle bells, jingle all the way," I warble with the radio, trying to soothe her. We drive through melting snow and abandoned dairy farms, we drive through tiny towns decked out in plastic ivy. "Oh what fun it is to ride in a one-horse open sleigh."

Ava will have none of it. I can tell she thinks "Jingle Bells" sucks. It isn't until we get to Utica and a CVS Pharmacy, where I can finally dose her with Tylenol and rub baby Ambesol all over her gums, that she finally gives it up and falls asleep, her head tilted forward so I can't see her face at all. I wonder how well she can breathe in that position. I am still new at babies.

Can they die from excessive crying? Do they ever have strokes? Do they seize?

I think of the wisdom of that trooper, who had kindly refrained from ticketing me. I find myself wishing he would stop us again, just to hear him talk about the problems he has with his baby. Just to hear a person talk at all and put my life into a perspective, any perspective.

I've lost that. What was it about Daddy coming and then leaving that set me off-kilter? It is as if the cloud he walked in has infected me, spawned a malaise I cannot name. I am swimming from moment to moment, trying to latch on to life again. To regain footing. To be sure about something.

chapter 11

Home Again

>------<∞H∞>------<

We have been going to Denny's for most of our meals these days—until the other night, when Ava threw a salt shaker at a waitress and clocked her between the eyes, dead center. Under our table was a sea of crumbs, silverware, and spilled milk. I apologized to the manager, who had rushed to the waitress's aid. People were staring, giving me that "Hey, lady, can't you control your own kid?" look.

"Maybe she isn't ready for dining out," the manager suggested, trying to be kind and uninvite us to return at the same time. I apologized again to him, to the waitress, to the people at the next table, thinking *dining* isn't exactly the word I would choose to describe eating at Denny's.

Afterward, Ava cried in the car and squirmed in her car seat as though it were a straitjacket. "It's okay, honey, it's okay," I comforted her. "We don't need their pancakes."

From that day on we have gone to eat at my friend Elliot's natural-food restaurant, the Whole in the Wall, instead. It is there I am reminded that Ava really loves other food besides pancakes, macaroni and cheese, and Cheerios, which I was feeding her almost exclusively. Now I remember she loves broccoli. She stuffs bunches into her mouth as fast as she can, as though I have been starving her of vitamins. People are staring again.

The waitresses at the Whole in the Wall are very nice. "She's so cute," says a beautiful girl, smiling at Ava, who is not, in fact, having one of her cuter moments. She has smeared milk and crumbs in her hair and has broccoli actually sticking to her forehead. She saves pieces in her balled-up fists and later I find a wad in the leg of her pants.

I think again of Alison's words: I am a single mother. I am beginning to understand what that means. We are a unique tribe of the hardy and desperate. We pillage packages of saltines from cafeterias, never knowing how tired we will be later and whether we will have energy to prepare a meal. We peel food out of our children's hair at night, alone, when they have finally fallen asleep. We fall asleep beside them fully clothed, abandoning the formalities of pajamas and cribs.

One night when we get home after eating at the Whole in the Wall, I realize that my answering machine still has Shane's voice on it and I change the message. "Ava and Elizabeth are not in," I say plainly. "Please leave a message."

It is simple. To the point. We are a mother and child, alone. There is something honest about it.

⊱─────⊰

But a mother and child alone we were not meant to be. A few months after my father leaves, it is decided he will return. Things aren't working out in Seattle.

"I can't do this, with Daddy here," my sister says on the phone. She writes me a pithy e-mail to explain. "I am having a breakdown."

I wonder what that is, a breakdown. How does one go about having one? Does it mean you get to rest? Have breakfast in bed? Play with your children all day? Take long baths with special relaxation-inducing salts or calming oils?

I want to have a breakdown, too. But someone has to take care of Daddy. With both daughters having breakdowns, who would do it? Besides, I don't really know how to go about it; the only thing I have ever broken down is cardboard boxes. To break down myself would be too complicated, and it might upset Ava. I simply don't have the energy, even for a minor collapse.

This time, recognizing that such a journey alone would be unduly stressful for Daddy, I fly with Ava to Seattle to get him. It is early January. Hanukkah and Christmas have come and gone. In Seattle there are gifts for Ava, gifts for me. Ava gets a giant Winnie the Pooh that talks. I shudder, trying to imagine hauling it back on the plane. We haven't brought anyone gifts.

Shane's mother, Elissa, brought the giant Pooh from where she lives, on Friday Harbor, outside of Seattle. She clucks her tongue and shakes her head when we talk about Shane. She doesn't understand it, it isn't the son she knows. She is "very disappointed," she says.

Elissa takes Ava home with her for three days. It was my idea, actually. I thought it would give me some time to rest and catch up with my mother and sister, and to gauge how Daddy is doing. And Ava would get to know her other grandmother. But the three days stretch out unbearably. The nights are even worse. Without her breathing and dreaming beside me, my own thoughts run wild. I can't sleep at all. My brain is frantic with unhappiness. I press the pillow against my face to muffle my sobs so I don't worry my family. For the first time I realize the usefulness of being constantly busy—you have no free time to think about things that are bothering you.

To chase away bad thoughts late at night, I lie on the couch in my sister's living room and get lost once again in reruns of *Baywatch* and infomercials on her large-screen television. I bask in its blue-orange glow for hours, like a woman at a temple. On my credit card I purchase a compilation CD of punk rock music, a Pocket Fisherman, a Ginsu knife set, and a machine that chops vegetables.

The next day I call Visa and cancel them.

Mommy, Daddy, and I go out to breakfast at a diner around the corner from my sister's house. But there is a problem. Daddy is having a lot of trouble deciding whether to eat pancakes or eggs. "Do I like those?" he asks my mother, who assures him he does, "with a little piece of bacon on the side."

When the food comes, he picks up his spoon and my mother takes it away, handing him a fork. She hands him the salt, which he has not asked for. They have a way of dealing with this illness, a silent pact. "Wipe your mouth," she says.

Together they have shared a cramped bedroom in my sister's house. Melanie is raising her two kids on a strict program of McDonald's Happy Meals and the threat of time-out punishments, which makes them a bit hyper. The whole arrangement isn't working very well. Especially with Daddy there. At night, he moves *her* papers now, rearranges *her* life. She isn't as tolerant.

"I have to go start a job out there with some people up North," Daddy says to my sister as we pack his clothes. My mother sits on the edge of their bed and weeps.

"That's right, Daddy, a job," I say, and feel the weight of the decision to bring him back press down on me, wondering what I have taken on.

The day before we leave, we go grocery shopping for my sister. Daddy gets lost in the store while looking for the tuna fish. He has misplaced our umbrella and it has begun to sprinkle. "Stupid," my mother whispers, beneath her breath. In the car, Daddy slumps beside us, his wet hair flattened against his head.

But when we unpack the bags at home, I see it beneath the tuna fish. The small blue umbrella. "Look, Daddy," I say, when my mother leaves the room, "the umbrella!"

"Oh good," he says, clapping his hands, as if we found a lost diamond ring or her heirloom watch. "We'll save it for her as a surprise."

On the plane home, Ava's ears begin to hurt. She is either cutting teeth again or has given herself an earache with her peculiar habit of putting the nipple of her bottle into her ear. She sneaks to do it, delights in the fact that I have made it forbidden. I'll catch her, lying down, eyes closed, her bottle neatly tucked into the side of her head.

Somewhere over Idaho, the pain crescendos with the altitude and she begins to clutch her ears and scream like a banshee, the way she did at Samme's house on Christmas Eve. This child has a scream on her that even Hollywood would envy. Only nobody is entertained by it. We are on a plane, surrounded by people. Annoyed people.

Daddy gets up and walks down the aisle. He walks back. Up and back. Up and back. He touches Ava's head. "What is wrong with him?" he asks.

"Teething," I say.

I explain that I left behind the baby's medicine. I wanted to travel light because I thought it would make things easier. I desperately wanted an easier time. But on the way to the airport I had a moment of sanity and asked my sister to stop at a drugstore so I could pick up Infants' Tylenol, baby Motrin, and Ambesol. "They have that in the airport," she said.

They did not, unfortunately, have it in *that* airport.

On the plane, a woman in front of us with a toddler asks if she can help. She gives me some Infants' Tylenol and a box of toys, which Ava flings into the air with fury. A *Toy Story* soldier hits an elderly man on the back of the head. He turns and scowls.

"Where am I going?" Daddy asks. "I am having something of a blackout. Perhaps you can remind me who you are?"

We get to Binghamton in a blizzard and are picked up by Gary Graham, the managing editor at the newspaper, and his wife, Jane. They are two of a handful of people that I have told about Shane leaving us and Daddy coming back. Now they have come out on an icy night to drive us home.

It is late, bone-chillingly cold, and moonless, and I am covered with the sticky residue of a cup of orange juice Ava overturned in my lap somewhere over Nebraska. We are all getting sore throats. I feel embarrassed when the neatly dressed couple sees us tumble off our plane.

When we get to our house, the Grahams go out to get us

some milk and bread. It is a long drive to the Hess gas station convenience store, and while they are gone I give Daddy a tour. I am carrying Ava, who has fallen asleep. We walk from room to room, opening and shutting doors.

"We are home," I say. "Remember this room?" I show him the bedroom I fixed up for him in August.

"Yes, this is where I was in the Army," he says. "Oh God, I am back."

After the trip from Seattle, Ava and I settle back into our room and Daddy into his again, the room with the slanted eaves he bumps his head on when he rises. Ava still sleeps with me, something I know that people frown upon. That evening, when we get home, she says, "Home, home, home, Mommy!" and she and I collapse into sleep together, exhausted. It makes me happy that she likes being home, as if home is a good place. A place she, at least, is glad to return to.

But soon after she goes down I hear a noise. It is Daddy going down the stairs, resuming his practice of sifting through things downstairs. I know I should go and talk to him, try to orient him, lead him back upstairs, but I can't. I can't move. My legs feel numb. My head is a slab of lead denting the pillow in half. I am paralyzed by exhaustion. Eventually he walks back upstairs and opens the door to our room. "Excuse me," he says. "I seem to be lost."

I lead him down the hall, hand him towels and soap and toothpaste. "This is your room. See here, it says your name, SANDY."

Anticipating his return, I'd resumed my project of putting

up signs with a vengeance. They are everywhere, on everything. Tina Hudock, a neighbor who sometimes watches Ava, has lent me a label gun that spits out stickered letters and I have made a science of labeling: SHOWER, LIGHT, BOOKS, STEP UP, STEP DOWN, DRAWER, LIGHT, WATER. I labeled Daddy's toothbrush. I labeled the toilet.

It reminds me of the time I had a roommate in college who was taking French. She, too, labeled our lives. Everything had a French word on it. "This is what they recommend," she said, "for the fastest absorption of language."

I do not expect Daddy to actually absorb language. I just want to remind him about things. And I'd like to keep him from peeing in the wastebasket.

"In the morning, I will show you where to get a nice hot shower, Daddy," I say.

"That's good. Real good. I need a shower because tomorrow I start my new job."

I tell him that is good. But he is retired. He doesn't have to work too hard.

His new job—what will it involve? he asks.

"We'll talk in the morning," I say. I go back in my room and turn on the television. I watch *Letterman* while the baby beside me snores like her father. Then I watch *The Late Late Show with Craig Kilborn*. Beautiful women come on and talk about their beautiful lives. Everyone is ironic.

Then the infomercials begin. There are new, exciting, post-Christmas consumer possibilities. Gone are the Ronco machines that chop and dice and scramble eggs in their shells. Now you can buy a Torso Tiger, which will make exercising your abs as easy as rolling out dough. You can buy a special appliance for facial exercises to prevent you from ever looking old. I lie in bed, worrying about Daddy and Ava and the animals and wondering if I should develop my abs and eliminate my wrinkles so I, too, can be beautiful and have a beautiful life.

Then I decide what my father's new job will be. And finally, I sleep.

chapter 12

The Memory Project

———◄◄◆◄◆►◆►►———

We are sick. We have been sick for days. Coughing, wheezing, sneezing, we sit in the emergency room with Ava at Wilson Memorial Regional Medical Center in Johnson City, waiting for someone to tell us why her temperature is 104. Daddy drinks machine coffee. It is 2:00 A.M.

He has been asking me over and over when his job starts. I decide to tell him: "Now, Daddy."

"Funny, I don't feel like a daddy," he says.

"You are. You are my father."

"Really? I know it sounds crazy, but I don't remember you at all."

The baby looks at him and blurts out: "Funny Pop-pop."

"Hey, that was almost a sentence," I say.

"Am I his father, too? Are you my mother?"

"No, Daddy, you are her grandfather. She is a girl. Her name is Ava. I am your daughter, Beth. Your mother is dead."

"She is?" he asks. "Everything is so confusing, it's all topsy-turvy, mishy-mashy-meshuggeneh in my head. Things get sort of muddled about or they get in order for a while and then disappear. Like my mother, when did she die?"

"I guess about forty years ago. I think you are talking about your wife, Julia."

"Oh yes! That's what I mean—Julia—she didn't die?"

"No."

"I can't explain this feeling inside my head. It's all so crazy, so wickety-whack."

"I know, Daddy," I say.

The nurse calls us in. Ava's temperature has dropped to 101; she has a double ear infection, probably from the leakage of the bottles she still insists on squeezing into her ears. We leave the hospital with her swaddled in blankets and a prescription for antibiotics that cannot be filled until morning. It is snowing hard.

"So what is it?" he asks.

"An ear infection."

"No, my job."

I tell him his job is to help me take care of things at the house. And to tell me a memory each night.

"Oh, so it is a sort of academic project," he says.

"Exactly," I say. "A memory project."

"Oh," he says. "Well, my memory isn't what it used to be."

Snow engulfs us on the drive home. The headlights shining a path through the thick, swirling flakes make me dizzy. It feels as though we are particles inside a blender. The snow is so thick and the space inside the car so close and tight and filled with humans breathing, I feel claustrophobic.

Sometimes I think forgetting is a virus, that if I am not careful I might catch it. In the cramped, wet, cold interior of the car in the snowstorm, the windows steaming up, I think Ava and I are breathing in Daddy's exhaled air. We are breathing in forgetfulness. It could be dangerous. In the car in the blizzard I could forget important things, like the way home.

When we get back the house is freezing. I turn up the heat, but the important *clunk* sound of the furnace igniting does not follow. "Hold her," I tell Daddy, handing him Ava. I go down to the cellar to look at the furnace. The light has burned out and I am out of bulbs. I shine a flashlight I have left on the stairs. Above me I hear the screech of Ava, who has awakened in my father's arms, and then the sound of Daddy, trying to comfort her.

The gauge on the fuel tank reads zero. Zero as in no fuel. Zero as in seriously fucked. I shine the flashlight around to see my way back to the wooden stairs. "Hey, hey, somebody," my father yells. "There is a problem. This baby has a problem."

The flashlight beam falls on something furry and white in a corner. For a moment I freeze. Could it be a rat, a cat, or maybe—I entertain for just a second—one of the invisible bears, crouched down, ready to spring? Too small. Too white. The bears would be black. Our cats are gray and orange. Rats have naked tails.

I take a step. Then another.

In the shadows of the basement an enormous, red-eyed, white rabbit stares at me. It is petrified, backed into a corner. We consider each other for a moment. "Coming, Daddy," I yell up.

The baby has squirmed out of his arms and is lying on the floor, writhing in anger and pain. "He is upset about something," Daddy says.

"She," I say. "She. Ava is a girl, Daddy. Get it? A girl. And she is sick."

I realize that we are experiencing what could be considered an emergency. The drive to our house was treacherous in the icy storm. We can't go back out. We have no heat. Ava is very sick.

"We have a problem, Daddy," I say. "We have to get two fires started very fast in the woodstove and the fireplace. We're out of heating oil."

Something about the situation appears to register deep inside him. Crisis hits a nerve. His eyes, normally cloudy, seem clear. "That wood on the porch looks dry," he says. "I saw old newspapers there in the hallway."

In fact, he is right. Someone has stacked a neat pile of dry wood on our porch and even left a smaller pile of kindling right by the door. Within fifteen minutes, Daddy has a fire blazing in the fireplace and another roaring in the woodstove. Heat begins to replace the air that was so chill we could see the white flags of our breath when we walked in. We huddle in blankets before the fire with Samo and all three cats, coughing and competing for the heat. Ava is burning with fever again. Daddy takes her from me and presses cool compresses, which he has prepared from toilet paper, on her face and chest. Beneath his hands she drops into sleep. Later he goes outside and brings in more armloads of wood.

As we sit in front of the fire, he says he is ready to start his new job, his memory project. He has some "memories available," he says. In the warm glow of the flames, cradling sleeping Ava, he tells me about the war, where he served in the Pacific Theater.

He speaks in a low voice, which is either to prevent waking Ava or because the subject matter deems it for him. "It was wet all the time. We slept in mud, in muddy tents," he says. "Just boys, all of us. Boys with guns." A tear slips down his nose.

He recounts the way the mud sucked at them, day and night, first on the island of Leyte and later on Bougainville, where they established a beachhead.

Then he shifts stories. He tells me about how he got sick. Daddy got malaria while he was in the Army. It was the reason he never drank alcohol. But now the name of the disease that lived in his body over sixty years ago has walked away from him. But the experience of it remains.

At night, Daddy says, he could hear the artillery fire in the hills. He could see it from his tent, it looked like distant lightning. "I couldn't eat. I turned yellow. There was no real kind of hospital. All the time I was shivering. I got a fever disease."

Although he was sick, he was expected to continue his job. He scouted for enemy gun emplacements, and he would go out in a small group at night or early dawn. "I was so cold and wet," he says. "They didn't have the right medicine.

"There was a splash. A *ka-splash,*" he says, raising his voice a bit. Sensing his excitement, Ava shifts in his lap. "I didn't know what it was; it was dark. I looked for my partners, the other guys, and they were all behind me or in front of me. Or on the other side."

He grows silent.

"What was it, Daddy?"

"What?"

"The splash.

"That was . . . it was . . . it was something we didn't see."

"Was it dangerous?"

"No. No. Not dangerous," he says. "I think it was frogs."

A private promoted to technical sergeant, Daddy got so sick that he was finally sent to a hospital in California. After that he went back to Cleveland, where his family lived still. I know this from my mother. But when I ask him, he shakes his head. "Don't know about any of that," he says. California and Cleveland and the end of the war are gone. All he has kept is its center, full of mud and frogs and fever.

We sit quietly for a while, listening to Ava's shallow breathing. I think about her fever, broken now, about when the phone lines will be up again and what it must be like to forget the end of a war.

As the blizzard roars outside, I stoke up the fire; he shivers, and I wonder if he may be getting sicker. And whether he can separate the chill of the night from the chill of his hepatitis-racked body sixty years ago. I decide to remind him. I say, "Daddy, good thing you got out of there. Good thing you made it."

"Yes. Not all the guys were that lucky."

"Yeah, and you got to go to college on the GI Bill. That was lucky, too."

Not meaning to, I have opened a door. I have cracked a sub-conscious code. I have accessed another memory. Daddy says, "And I had a great professor. One of the good ones."

He tells me about this teacher, a woman named Alma Herbst. He is so pleased when her name comes right to him, without a second's delay. A chip of iron flying to a magnet. "She had a tick, she always tilted her head like this, just so, and she enunciated every letter of every word. She was brilliant. She was the one who encouraged me. I was sort of her pet, and then later on she was my buddy."

Herbst must have gotten him on the academic path he was to take, to study labor and industrial relations. It was a path that would take him to jobs with the government, serving on the Wage Stabilization Board of the late 1950s, in Bolivia—advising the government on currency and industrial relations—in the 1960s, and later to teaching positions at Butler University, the University of Illinois at Urbana-Champaign, and finally to his tenured position at the University of New Mexico. That is where he would write a history of the American labor movement, which he dedicated to her on the first page: *To Alma Herbst.*

Where is Alma Herbst now? She would be very old. Maybe she, too, has this disease of forgetting. She may have passed away, but she is alive tonight in Daddy's mind, a woman who has appeared to him in great detail in a snowstorm as he cradles a sick child more than half a century later.

My father is small, about five-feet-seven. Once he was almost handsome, eyes shining with intelligence, and a confident half smile. He has a small but visible gap between his two front teeth. Now he is balding with wisps of gray hair; his once bright eyes are remote and dark as stones in water. He must have begun losing his hair a long time ago, because when I was in my twenties I wrote a poem about a family outing in which I described him and my mother like this:

> *My father's bald spot shines like a yarmulke,*
> *my mother wears an illness like a beautiful new dress.*

That bald spot has claimed much of his pate; he is very frail, and his weight hovers around 110. But on this cold night of reclaimed memories, he seems larger, stronger. Something inside him seems focused and present. Part of him has come back tonight, to help me get through the storm.

"Beth?" Daddy calls out when I am in the bathroom.

"Be right there," I yell back.

"Get some more cool pads."

He is still holding Ava, her head buried in his chest.

"There is a rabbit in the basement," I say.

"How about that! Isn't that something?" he says. The rest of the night, while I doze on the couch with Ava on my chest, he keeps the fire roaring, he keeps us warm.

———◦◦※◦◦———

It seems as though my father has returned from a long journey, far away. There is a look of success in his eyes, like he has recently done something marvelous. For three days he speaks to me with clarity, sobriety; he addresses me by name, seems to recognize Ava. He asks when the men from Economy Heating will deliver the heating oil, and he answers the door when they come. He asks what happened to the rabbit, how Mommy is doing.

"The rabbit is gone," I say. "I guess it got out itself. And Mommy is sick, Daddy. Her heart is weak."

"Shouldn't I be there with her?" he asks, concerned.

"No, it's okay. She has a lot of help from Melanie and her doctors."

"Oh," he says dejectedly.

He sweeps the kitchen, brings me a pile of his clothes to

wash. Seeing Daddy so changed makes me sad in a new way. I cannot stand the thought of him reverting. I want him to be just like this for the rest of our lives.

I make an appointment for Daddy to get a dementia evaluation with our family doctor, Frank Eder. I want to know how bad it is, and why his mind can leave and return like this. I want to know how I can make it stay.

Daddy's excited about the appointment. "We will be able to put this Alzenheimer theory to rest," he says.

"That would be good," I respond.

At work they have given me a column. Once a week I can write about anything I want. It's to be called "Close to Home." I wrote the first one about moving to the old house on Beartown Road. I have now written another one about living with Daddy and Ava. I write in the column about how strange it seems to be with them. It is as though the three of us comprise a parabola— the beginning, middle, and end of life. Ava is in her first year, I am in my fortieth, and Daddy, his eightieth. I feel as though I am poised at the center of what it means to be alive, caring for life's two extremities. Ava is where I have been and Daddy is where I am going. That is a scary thought to eat breakfast with.

Then, just as I feared, before his appointment with Dr. Eder Daddy begins to fade away again.

"What was that word . . . ?" he asks. "You know, the clear and white stuff that encrusted on the tip of the stairs outside."

"Ice?"

"Yes, yes, that's it!"

Ava—ever listening—exclaims, "Ice! Ice!"

Daddy walks around now this way, dropping pieces of language behind him, the baby following, picking them up. He asks for "the liquid substance from the spigot." She asks for "wawa." He wants a tissue to wipe his "blowing device." She says, "Wipe, Mommy," and points to her runny nose.

She points to her scabbed knee and says, "Owchy knee." She points to the tiny white nub that has emerged from her gums and says, "Owchy toof!"

And when Daddy sits speechless at breakfast, picking at an egg he clearly has no interest in, Ava tells me, "No egg, no egg, no egg! Mommy! Nana!"

She wants a banana. I give it to her, and she hands Daddy a piece. They sit side by side and share the banana. The two of them get along well. Every morning now she slides off the bed and runs into his room, pushing open his door and saying, "Pop-pop!"

"Hello there, little guy," he says.

I have to wipe Ava's face after eating—she smears the food all over herself. Daddy has bits of food on his face after eating, too. Ava wants to try to zip up her coat. "Sipsipsip," she says. Daddy can no longer engage the zipper on his coat. I zip them up each morning, and we go out to walk Samo.

Then Daddy asks me to write down the name of the disease. "That thing I have."

I write it on a napkin: *Alzheimer's*.

He takes the napkin from me very carefully, like an important document. He folds it in half. Then he puts it in his shirt pocket, next to his heart, as if by holding on to its name he could manage, somehow, to keep the disease at bay.

Usually we walk up and down our road, but this week someone has plowed out the cemetery, so we trek through it and read the gravestones. The walk is the first we've taken in more than a week, and it feels great to simultaneously breathe the crisp, cold air and bask in the warm sun. We walk in the ruts of the snow-plow trucks; our six feet and four paws engrave tracks in the snow. As we pass by the woods, deep and peaceful with a few birds twittering above, I think of the bears of Beartown Road, our other neighbors, somewhere nearby. We are a part of this place. We belong here. Our footprints look right on the path, atop the tire treads, familiar as the torn wire fence and grave-stones, familiar as the clouds.

I read that sunlight is good for people with Alzheimer's dis-ease. I believe it. Daddy is always more lucid in the sun. As we walk in the graveyard he makes astute comments about the peo-ple buried there.

"The Spanish-American War, what a thing! All these kids over here died in that!" He is incredulous.

The Civil War. The Revolutionary War. The world wars. "Now, those were wars," he says.

The boys who died in the wars have names like Darius and Elijah.

"Now, those are names!" Daddy says.

At night, after the sun goes down, he drifts away.

<hr>

I take Daddy to see Dr. Eder. He examines him thoroughly—listens to his heart, looks in his ears, nose, and eyes. He gives him a mental test called the Mini-Mental State Examination (MMSE). It takes half an hour. He has to count backward from ten, say the months in reverse order, draw a clock. When I go into the examining room, Daddy tells me he has taken a comprehensive scholastic exam that is required of everyone in the nation. "It contains a rendition of opera," he says. "Falstaff, I think."

"That's called word salad," Dr. Eder says. It is very common for Alzheimer's patients.

"So he has it?" I ask Dr. Eder.

"I think we can go with that for now," he says.

"I do have it, Doc?" Daddy asks, shocked. He has maintained all along that he is fine, just having some minor memory issues.

"Yes, Mr. Cohen. You didn't do very well on the exam. The sorts of mistakes you made, the kinds of things you have been saying, they are examples of things people with this disease say."

"Like what?"

"Well, when I asked you what year it is, you said 1975. When I asked you the month, you said 1982. That means not only do you not know that this is 2000, but you do not remember the difference between year and month, a difference of category. I would say the disease is quite advanced."

My father looks stricken. "How long do I have, Doc?" he asks.

Dr. Eder explains to Daddy that he could live a very long time, but that as time goes on he will forget more and more things. "There are drugs that are believed to slow this down, but not much at the stage you're at," he says. He puts Daddy on high dosages of vitamin E and continues him on the drug Aricept. Then he asks me to come alone into his office.

"You are taking care of him, with the baby, too?"

"Yes."

"Husband?"

"Not present at this time."

"I see. Well. Number one, never leave him alone, and if you do, no cigarettes or matches, there is a serious fire risk. It happens all the time. Number two, you need to get some help."

I tell Dr. Eder that support groups never really worked for me. He says he means with Daddy's care. Daddy will never get better, he says. "He'll have good days and bad days. Treat him like a four-year-old, that's what he is now. Would you leave a four-year-old home alone?"

"No."

"Would you give a four-year-old matches?"

"No."

"That's how you should treat him."

Dr. Eder says that it would be good to keep Daddy busy. Daddy needs clocks and calendars, signs and symbols, points of reference. I should write pertinent information on sheets of paper for him.

I tell Dr. Eder about the memory project. How we go over one set of memories each night. "Could that help him, that sort of thing?" I ask.

"I don't know, couldn't hurt. Just be aware it's a progressive illness. It might not be today or tomorrow or this week, but he will go downhill. He will get worse. And you need to start thinking about what you are going to do then."

In the car, on the way home, my father cries. "I am dying," he says, "of this Alzenheimer's! I want a cigarette."

"It isn't fatal, Daddy. You could live a long time. You will just forget things."

"That's the same thing as being dead," he says.

I reach across the car and put my hand on Daddy's. Staring out the window at the white hills, without turning toward me he clutches my wrist with his hand, cold and damp with fear. He holds fast, even when I have to shift gears. He holds my hand until we get home, as if letting go would mean spinning away faster into a forgetting place neither one of us can bear to see him go.

chapter 13

Snowplow Angels

————◦◦ ◦◦————

It is snowing again. Feet and feet are piling up. The back door won't open. The accumulation in the driveway is so deep, it is impossible to pull out. We are stranded, our house is an island in a snow sea.

I hear the roar of snowplows early in the mornings, before dawn. They sound ravenous and important. The county sends them to clear the roads, which they do well. But there is a problem. In the task of clearing, they create steep mountains of snow alongside the road that block me even farther in the driveway. The snowy mounds reach four or five feet high and are impossible to back through or even walk around. They melt and then harden, trapping us in a cage of ice. I go out and battle them with a shovel. But I need a pick, or an ax. Something sharp to bite through the rock-hard places of frozen plowed snow. It takes hours.

Some days, after the snowplows pass, I hear smaller engines, purring furiously. The forward gears are high-pitched, a middle C of motion. The backward gear is lower. G-flat, perhaps. A grumbling.

The neighbors have come. They have figured it out: Shane has left. They know Daddy is here, because I have written about it in my new column. They have seen us bundled up, taking walks before the big snows hit. Ava, Daddy, Samo, and me.

One morning I peek out the slotted window in the guest bedroom to identify the machine at work in front of our house. There is Mr. Wright, in a neon-orange snowsuit, upon his riding lawn mower with its snowplow attachment, making a neat path out the drive. He even does the walkway.

I consider waving to him but change my mind. There is a reason for the predawn mission; it is as if he wants to spare me the embarrassment of gratitude. Or himself the awkwardness of explaining, or saying what must be obvious. That I need help.

It is not the first time this has happened. The other morning I spied Jerry Lainhart, a retired Vietnam veteran from the next parcel of land, with his son Vaughn, outside shoveling. They made a path to the door, too, and one to the woodpile. And Ralph Hudock comes over regularly with his son, Andy. They live in an old trailer back behind the Lainharts'. They come in the afternoon, with their snowblower, while I am at work. Once, I came home early and there they were. We greeted one another, but they never really looked at me. In fact, seeing me sent them into a fever pitch of shoveling. They'd been caught, red-handed, in a pique of altruism. And although I can't prove it, I think it was they who moved some wood onto the porch one day when I was out. I recognized Ralph's big boot prints in the snow—he is a giant of a man.

As though to spare me shame, these people come silently.

When we come home from errands or a doctor's appointment or day care, the driveway will be shoveled. The porch will be salted. When we awake in the morning, the drive will have been plowed anew, a pathway shoveled to the mailbox.

There is an unspoken credo of helping on Beartown Road. It is as if, here, we are anchored to another century. To a time when helping was the rule, not the exception. A time when a neighbor's help could mean survival.

Because so often we do not see our benefactors, it sometimes seems like we have been assigned a troop of forest elves to look after us. They are stealthy, the way they come and go.

Help is a lovely thing. The very thought of it warms me. I realize how often I have been on its receiving end. Although I have taken care of people's children, cooked meals for them in crises, given money and time to various causes, mostly I have played the role of helped one in my life. I have received gifts and scholarships. Umbrellas in the rain. Taxis in Manhattan stopped for me at all hours, even when their white lights were off. Once, when I was eight months pregnant, a bus going off-duty stopped for me and drove me all the way home, right to the door of my building. I was the only one on the bus. The driver told me knock-knock jokes.

But in the past I have always seen my angels. This is different. Are notes of thanks expected? Should I confront the people who help us, make them confess to their philanthropy? Should I be embarrassed that they think I am so lame? Should I bake cookies? Banana bread? Cakes? And when would I do that? I haven't baked in months.

I wonder sometimes why they do it. How can they take the time from their own lives? These are not wealthy people. They have their own struggles. I have never seen anything like their generosity of spirit. I imagine the sweat on their foreheads, veins standing out, as they shovel away in our yard. Do they plan their helping missions? Are there meetings or phone calls among them, figuring out schedules?

I use my job at the paper to thank them. I write a column about neighbors. I write about kindness.

At work I have rearranged my cubicle to reflect the changes in my life. I take down a picture of Shane and put up one of Daddy and Ava.

I have started to write about my own life all the time: about snow, about memory, about loss. About Alzheimer's. Writing gives me a sense of control. It has its own special alchemy. I can make what is terrible turn beautiful, like our purple-gray shadows on the snow.

I write about the cemetery across from Beartown Road. The babies and old people buried there. Daddy, Ava, and I crunch through the snow reading their headstones. They lived—some of them—a century ago.

The cemetery makes me realize that Daddy is not the only one with Alzheimer's disease. The whole world has it. Who were these people? These Crockers and Holcombs, Villecos and Moots? The roads here are named after them; some of their relatives still live on them. Linda, who works at the tiny Tunnel Post Office, is a Holcomb. I ask her about specific people buried in the cemetery. She does not know who they were. I may know more than she does just from reading the headstones.

What were these people like? How did they fare the winters? Who remembers them? Sometimes I think nobody does. They have disappeared the same way my name has become erased from Daddy's mind. They were caught up in an obscuring mist, like the one that embraces the valley and hills of Colesville so many mornings, rendering everything invisible. They have vanished.

There were native people here, too, long before the Holcombs, Villecos, Crockers, and Moots. They lived along these rivers and in these hills, they hunted and trapped, fished and foraged. Maybe they even ate blackberries off of the same bushes that grow wild all over our property. They had children. They grew old. Tribes like the Algonquin, the Onondaga, the Tuscarora, and the Iroquois are believed to have inhabited the area. I imagine their babies played like Ava does. They put their plump hands out into the snowy nights and laughed when they felt the flakes melt upon their warm baby skin. They threw their heads back like she does, to let the flakes fall upon their tongues.

Like Ava now, their babies must have learned about the world. At night she has invented her own ritual. She looks out the window and says, "Night-night moon. Night-night star. Night-night sky. Night-night tree. Night-night house. Night-night kitties. Night-night Samo."

I can imagine the Iroquois babies engaged in the same ritual. Bidding good night to the world. Their elders probably sat quietly by firesides and told stories, remembered what they could of earlier years, like Daddy does. While their infants marveled at what was, they tried to hold on to what had been.

They are even more completely vanished; not even headstones in the cemetery mark their passing.

If Ava is life's beginning, if I am its center and Daddy is its final chapters—then these forgotten people are its postscript. Archaeologists may dig up their campsites, they may reassemble their baskets, arrowheads, and pottery, reconstruct their hunting patterns, but we will never know their names. They are the end of history, when history itself disappears.

chapter 14

Naming the Continents

━━━━━◄◦◦⋈◦◦►━━━━━

Not only are there snowplows, snowblowers, and shovelers that come before dawn: Someone has begun placing packages of food on our doorstep when we aren't around. The food is neatly wrapped and home-cooked. Meat loaf, mashed potatoes, and green beans. Lasagna. Pot roast and stewed carrots. One package comes wrapped in wax paper, another, aluminum foil. Other times it is neatly placed inside someone's much-used Tupperware or on a paper plate, covered with cellophane. I nuke it in the microwave, and we eat like real people. Daddy says, "Now, this is what I call a meal."

Ava concurs: "Ummy."

The food is better than what I usually make: hot dogs, and macaroni and cheese, and spaghetti. But I feel guilty. There are people who are actually starving who could use this food. Do we really qualify for bona fide charity? Still, there is something so nice about coming home to a house with dinner waiting. It reminds me of my childhood, my mother's perfect meals, which came complete with cloth napkins rolled into napkin holders.

It is great to have food sent, from someone, somewhere, but I am starving in a different way now. For logic and conversation. Ava is moving toward these things and Daddy away from them. I feel lonely sometimes, even in their company. Sometimes I talk to myself.

When I least expect it, a different kind of angel appears. Her name is Jody Hackett. She worked at Ava's old day care and had told me she'd once been a nanny for a couple in England. She said she would like to be one again someday.

On a chill Saturday morning she calls our house. She says she has just had foot surgery and will be getting married shortly, but she'd love to work for me. I tell her I need a nanny, but there is a complication. I tell her about Daddy.

"I had a grandparent with Alzheimer's," she says. "It's not a problem." She says she can watch Ava and Daddy. And she can cook. She loves to cook. She is twenty-three. She is enthusiastic. Jody Hackett sees our lives as a puzzle she wants to help solve.

Immediately, she takes away Ava's pacifiers ("She's too old") and introduces the sippy cup ("Bottles are gross"). She makes Daddy smoke outside, and he has to put on a coat and scarf. The exhaled smoke mixes with the steam of his breath in the cold. Sometimes, if the baby is asleep, I go out there and smoke with him; it makes me dizzy, but it gives us a sort of camaraderie. "It isn't really worth it, is it?" he says when we come back in and shake off the snow on our boots.

Life is clearing, suddenly easier. While I am at work, Jody makes chicken and biscuits and brownies. She does the laundry.

When I come home, dinner is ready, the house is neat, there are no papers carpeting the floors. No objects out of their places. The toilets are flushed.

After dinner, Daddy and I play with Ava. She is learning how to count. She says, "One, two, three, one, two, three, one, two, three," and then "Get me, Mommy," as she runs away. She has gone from toddling to a sort of unstable running. Now she is reinventing the game of tag.

After we play and I put her to bed, Daddy and I stay up awhile to talk about his memories. Sometimes I give him quizzes I know he'll pass. It makes me feel good.

"What was once referred to as the Dark Continent?"

"Africa."

"Down under?"

"Australia."

"Where we live?"

"Cleveland."

"No, Daddy, the continent."

"Oh, the United States."

"That's our country!"

"Oh."

"We live in North America."

"Right."

I am giving Daddy's brain an exercise class. I drill him like a sergeant, make him do brain push-ups. Maybe I can get his mind back into shape. It is not unlike the experience of reading one of Ava's books with her, the ones with the pictures that she identifies.

"What is that, Ava?"

"Boy."

"And what is he holding?"

"Ball."

"What is he doing?"

"Ball."

"Is he playing with his dog?"

"Ball."

She wants to hold the book herself. She wants to be the one asking the questions. She asks me, "Mommy, what?" and points.

"A boy, playing with his dog and a ball," I say.

"Good, Mommy."

Once I had a friend with two brothers, whose father taught them geography when they were children by "giving" each of them parts of the world. He gave one the Pacific Ocean, one the Atlantic Ocean, and one the Indian Ocean. He gave them great rivers, in Russia and China and the United States. My friend said it worked, they all learned the Earth by the time they were ten.

I try to give my father rivers and continents. I want to find a way to help him locate himself on the East Coast, in central New York. Every day he asks me where he is. I say, "Daddy, today, remember the Hudson River. You just need to remember one thing all day. It is a very big river and runs right down into New York City."

"Okay," he says. "The Hudson River, the Hudson River,"

But when I ask him about it later, he has forgotten.

Then I get an idea. I take a plastic globe lamp and put it in his room. I put a piece of red tape on western New York, approximately where we live. "This," I tell him, "is where we are."

He puts his finger on the tape and turns the globe around and around. "This is nifty, it is a globe and illuminates."

"It is a lamp."

"And here we are!"

"Yes."

"Sort of a northeastern region."

"Exactly!"

I take a moment to congratulate myself. I have given my father central New York.

⊷⊶⊷⊷◆◆H◆◆⊷⊷⊶⊷

I've been looking for answers. Through a network of friends and journalism associates I find out about a state-funded adult day care program for people with Alzheimer's that is run in a church. Then I realize it is the same one that the social workers told me about. It is called GROW. It only costs fifteen dollars a day. I enroll Daddy two days a week to give Jody a break. The two days quickly morph into three.

It is one of the many new efforts I am making. I decide to try harder at being a family; to do better for Daddy and Ava. But it's a challenge, trying to find a way to climb back into the world. For months I have been sinking in a swamp of gloom. I am tired all the time. I have put on ten pounds. Each day I go through the motions of life, but that is about all. Aside from our Cole Park walks, each day since Shane left I do what needs to get done and that is it. Then I collapse into an orgiastic stupor of bad television.

All my dreams—for my family, for my husband, for myself, about fixing up the house, maybe having another child—have been aborted. In their place are the daily rituals of getting by. Ava and Daddy need to eat. They need clothes. They need baths.

As for me, I sometimes feel I hardly exist. It is a logical extrapolation. If I existed, truly, in any important or significant way, then how could my husband have left me?

In my shrinking life, I have done away with anything that isn't essential. Gone are my beautiful dresses and silk shirts (too much trouble going to the dry cleaner). Forget about makeup. Who has time? I run a brush through my hair once a day. I avoid all reflecting surfaces. Even windows.

I have a new way I think about Shane. I focus on his shortcomings. The way he listed about the house, like a ship in unsteady waters. I remind myself how he stumped out his cigarettes in the yard, leaving a trail that marked his days. He never, I am sure, wiped a table in his life. But in the midst of these meditations on his shortcomings, I get wistful. In spite of myself, I miss the strains of unplugged Nirvana that wafted from his studio, intoxicating as just-baked cinnamon bread. Sometimes, at night, I sit in his dark studio just to smell the uncapped oil paints and stale cigarette air. Though I order myself to hate him, it is as arousing as a first kiss.

But I know I can't mope around forever. I've allowed things to deteriorate dangerously. With Jody helping, giving me a little room to breathe, I am trying to get a grip. I must inject a little civility and sanity into our lives, if for no other reason than to save Ava and Daddy.

Somewhere in a magazine I read about the Mozart effect. Researchers have linked the listening of Mozart to intelligence. So I play a Mozart CD for Ava and Daddy every time we get in the car. I take her swimming during family hour at the YWCA. She cries when it's time to get out.

I buy tickets for Daddy and me to classical music concerts and plays at the Cider Mill Playhouse. Jody or a neighbor watches Ava so I can get him out of the house. Stuck inside with me, depressed, is no way to end, or begin, a life.

I have also begun to take Daddy to a therapist named William Connor. Every Saturday morning at eleven we drive to his office, where there is a deep sectional couch and a lot of books. Dr. Connor is portly, middle-aged, and Unitarian, a man with a framed Ph.D. on his wall. He frequently goes to conferences. When I call him to make appointments, sometimes he'll say, "I'll be in Atlanta that week for an annual meeting." He went to Europe to some sort of convention on depression. He keeps up with current trends in his field.

I think Dr. Connor might be just the person to help Daddy. I explain to him that Daddy is depressed. How he told me one day he feels locked in a box that is shrinking.

Dr. Connor nods. He takes notes on a yellow legal pad. His office has a lot of knickknacks. While I am talking, explaining our situation, Ava picks up a marble egg and tosses it onto the carpet, digs into a tiny tray holding his calling cards, and then splays them around the table. Then she lunges for a delicate wire sculpture. After our first visit to Dr. Connor with Daddy, Ava and I are politely invited to wait in the waiting room. This annoys me, because I want to hear what Dr. Connor says. He has told me he will concentrate on discussing ways Daddy can enjoy the rest of his life.

But the waiting room suits Ava fine. This is because there are fish. She pushes her nose against the tank and talks to them. "Hi, blue fish. Hi, green fish. Hi, Mommy fish. Hi, baby fish. Hi, Pop-pop fish."

I can't help but notice there is no Daddy fish.

Dr. Connor says one thing that can help Daddy is physical

activity, so we start going on our walks more often. Our favorite is the walk down Beartown Road to the end and back again. The paved gravel road has a steep hill on it, and when we walk up it Daddy says, "What an incline, I can feel all those cigarettes right now."

I wonder if he is really remembering them. Cigarettes smoked in his old office at the university, where books were piled in teetering stacks; cigarettes lit in the living room in our house in Albuquerque; cigarettes in restaurants and at cocktail parties that my mother dragged him to, because she was a party person even though he was not. Perhaps all the cigarettes of his life blur together into one symbolic cigarette, always smoked to the very tip, until his fingers yellowed. Smoking, apparently, is not easy to forget.

Unlike my name.

I try not to let it bother me. Every day now I have to introduce myself to Daddy anew, and then introduce Ava. I think he recognizes us as people he should know; we are not strangers. But our precise identities have flown away from him—we are birds that have migrated. We come back every now and then but always leave again.

Some afternoons I call my mother. I try to talk to her about Daddy. I tell her about Dr. Connor, about our walks, concerts we've gone to, swimming, Mozart, and Jody Hackett. I am gushing, manic. I want us to connect.

"He might be getting worse," I say. "We just can't tell."

My mother says she wants to change the subject, she wants to hear positive things. She asks me to stick to those. She wants to know what sort of food Jody cooks.

"Mom," I say, "I just think you should know about Daddy."

I tell her he loses control of his bowels from time to time. I tell her he can't remember my name. I tell her these things not to depress her but because I want her to offer me some suggestions. I want her help. She is my mother.

But when I talk about Daddy she sighs, hard. She becomes brittle. "Your father," she says, "never knew your name. He wasn't interested in children."

I keep talking to her even after we hang up. "He was, too," I say.

The problem when someone loses his memory is that people start reinventing him. They have their own versions. And you can't ask the person who is forgetting for help. They become a disputed territory.

I start looking through boxes. I want my version—the Daddy I remember—to be the real one. I have kept old letters, but I can't find any from him. I read my old diaries. I read about the time I went to Israel with my father when I was thirteen, right after my Bas Mitzvah. It was an awkward trip; we didn't know exactly how to be together, what sorts of things to talk about. But of course he knew my name. He had to have known it, to get through customs, to check into the hotel.

Finally I find it. Across from the contents page of *Issues in Labor Policy,* a book he edited in 1977, he lined up our names in a single column, like a grocery list.

To:

Julia

Beth

Melanie

The book must have belonged to my sister once, because he had also inscribed it. In his familiar jagged handwriting he wrote: *To Melanie—For years of fun and love—Daddy.*

My father had known our names. It was my mother who was not interested in children. I realize that she cannot allow him to forget us. It is much better if he never cared about us at all.

I take Daddy's book with me into the dank, stale-smoke chill of Shane's studio. It is freezing in there. There is ice on the floor. There must be a leak in the roof.

Like a blind person, I run my fingers over the pages of *Issues in Labor Policy.* I want to feel the pages in the dark that way, because in that book he is still and will always be the other Daddy, smart Daddy, before Daddy. I touch the soft paper as if brilliance were braille or sunshine or sex, something that goes in through your skin and ends up in your heart.

chapter 15

Losing and Keeping

When we go on our walks in the park, the dog gallops alongside us. He makes occasional forays into the snowy bushes, chasing something, probably rabbits. I love our walks.

Just as Daddy is closing down, tuning out, Ava is expanding, opening up to more and more of the world. Daddy gets very involved with the buttons on his coat; Ava wants to touch the trees, the snow, the ground. She wants to chase the rabbits, too.

When we get back to the car, I see she has picked up pieces of stick and rock, and instead of putting them in her mouth— her modus operandi six months ago—she now waves them in her tight fists and sometimes thrusts them down her pants. She shoves her hands deep into the snow and pulls up debris like treasure. I find it later, stuffed into her diaper—damp, dark loam that folds into the creases of her. She wants to keep our walks, take them home with her, save them for later.

On Sunday mornings we have begun to follow our Cole Park routine, the one Ava and Samo and I developed when

Daddy was back in Seattle. We drive about ten minutes from our house, up the road from Sanitaria Springs, a tiny hamlet on a stream at the exit from I-88.

What was good about Cole Park before Daddy came back was that it erased loneliness. We would go there, and the distance from town, the solitude, the cold, our abandoned state all became good things. We were hardy; we could do anything.

The first time I went there, with Ava and Samo, it was growing dark, and we just sat at the edge of the frozen lake. I had briefly considered walking out upon the lake ice to the center and lying down with Ava in the white expanse. There was something inviting about all that emptiness, the sense of danger, that the ice might crack and swallow us whole. It felt then like something we could do with very little interruption of the world, disappear silently between slabs of thick lake ice. It was not a sad thought. It seemed peaceful.

Geese skidded across the sky, and the dog bounced through the brush and barked at them. I tried to point the geese out to Ava—their loud honking combined with the dog's interest seemed like it should be enough to catch her attention—but she was obsessed with her mittens. She didn't like them and kept pulling them off and throwing them on the ground. The focal point of her universe hadn't moved that far out yet.

Now, in just a few months, she has completely changed. She mimics the slightest hum of a faraway train. A hawk circling above the freeway when we are driving makes her coo and point. She notices everything. To the new moon, a sliver peeking from behind a cloud, she waves and says "Hi, moon!" Echoing the wind in the trees, she says "Shhhh." I have to pull her away from the side of the road, where she becomes engrossed in a pile of rocks. She punches my arm and screams, "My rocks! Mine!"

The jaunts with Daddy and Ava to Cole Park are active. We have to keep moving or he gets too cold. He is so thin now, I can see his ribs, and there appears to be no flesh on the bones of his legs. So we walk quickly, down to the end of the lake, up through the trees on a path, and back to the car. The beauty of Cole Park is that nobody is ever there, so Samo can go leashless and free and he bounds with exuberance. Yet the park is stark and almost dreary, and Daddy says so. "Never had much of a taste for the outdoors," he says.

Without him the cold lake had seemed a noble landscape. Ice cloaked the branches of trees in clear jackets; there was so much sky. With Daddy along, the landscape looks more desolate than noble, and we seem like desperate characters set against it. A lake, a baby, an old man, a dog, and a woman.

Daddy complains all the way, mostly about the cold, the unpleasantness of the outing, the weather. But every time we go, he admits after the walk that he feels better. Basking in the sunlight, walking down the frosty hill, seeing the dog shoot arcs of powder into the air with his back legs, all have the effect of clearing his mind a bit.

I hope it feels good to him on some level. Lately he grows angry and confused at the slightest provocation. He is more aware he is losing his memory. He can feel it spilling, as though there were a hole in the back of his head. I think the awareness is a particular curse.

And his forgetting goes beyond the learned world. I can see now how he is losing more than his train of thought, the way to the bathroom, the names of the continents. He loses his balance. He loses his appetite. He loses his breath.

On our way home from our walks we go to Mac's Country Store, a small place frequented by hunters. We stamp our feet at the doorway until all the snow falls off, and we walk into the muggy warmth inside.

Having squirmed and moaned and whimpered enough, by the time we hit Mac's, Ava is ready to rock and roll. She roams the aisles, pulling out boxes of cereal and rolls of toilet paper, which I, following behind her, replace. It makes Daddy nervous how she touches things in the store. I tell him, "Daddy, this is what babies do, they make messes, we clean them up."

"What do you mean we, Kemo Sabe?" he says.

At Mac's, Ava demands a plastic bat and ball, encased in two hard sheaths of plastic, stapled together. The set costs twenty dollars, which seems high for such a cheap toy, but the pleasure she has derived from it since is well worth it. The bat is of no interest to her whatsoever. But the ball and the plastic sheaths she plays with for hours. She names the ball "Babo" and the plastic sheaths "Pumpum."

Together they bump talking Po the Teletubbie, bouncing Tigger, and singing Barney way down in the pecking order of her toys. She loves the word *ball* and has her own special inflection: "Bawl!" "Babo Bawl!" Daddy is the first to notice it. He is the one who seems to understand her the best. It is a word she says all the time now, whenever she sees anything round, including the pupils of our eyes. Ava throws Babo across the room and then chases it, for hours at a stretch.

She demands I let her sleep with Babo and Pumpum and cries when I take the stiff, sharp plastic away.

Ava likes to keep all sorts of things you would normally throw out. The plastic wrappers her diapers come in, the boxes of her new shoes, the tags off new clothes. I have to fight her over the stub ends of celery and carrots. She wants to take them back to her room, where she lines them up in rows on the wood floor and talks to them in baby gibberish. Then she tucks them in bed and bids them good night. They have names. They get sleepy and hungry. I find her trying to feed a piece of an old cookie to a chewed ear of corn she's pilfered from the dinner table.

Sometimes, when she is asleep, I find buttons, crayons, coins, and pieces of cookie clutched tight in her fist or stuffed down into her diapers; I have no idea where she gets them. She makes numerous piles of small items—a block, a piece of a puzzle, a bottle nipple, a ball, or a cracker. I find them all over the house. At fifteen months she is like a little mouse, storing and saving, as if afraid that all good things will be removed from her if discovered.

Her greatest passion is for Cheerios. I find them stuck in the mouths of all her stuffed animals and dolls. I find them in her books, placed meticulously atop the mouths of the characters in the illustrations. I find them in shoes, socks, and pockets. Once, I found one in her ear.

Cheerios, once they have been sucked on and spat out, become petrified, compact and hard as pebbles. They have a remarkable sticking power. They adhere to walls, books, clothes— anything.

The other morning I saw my father struggling with a sweater. Four fossilized Cheerios were stuck on the sleeve, which he was trying furiously to button into the buttonholes on the front of the sweater. "Those aren't buttons, Daddy," I said. "They're Cheerios."

"Oh."

A minute later I saw him trying to button them up again, making a twisted puzzle of the sweater. I came over and pulled them off, one by one.

"Thank you," he said. "I don't know why you are so nice to me."

———◄◦◦H◦◦►———

Because they lived through the Great Depression, both my parents were hoarders. My father always hoarded books, thoughts, ideas. My mother, everything else. She kept (and still keeps) plastic bottles, plastic bags, used tinfoil, bags, pins, boxes, buttons, pennies, and leftover food. Their refrigerator was always filled with packages of leftovers wrapped in the recycled tinfoil. Old biscuits, cheese, fruit with a piece cut from it, noodles, meats—all were meticulously wrapped and stashed in their refrigerator for months, until a cleaning lady periodically pried it all out and threw it away.

My mother has always put things in little piles, not unlike Ava. She enjoys keeping and having, sorting and piling up. She is the sort of woman who will hide a hundred dollar bill in a pocket of an overcoat for a rainy day.

Daddy hoarded something entirely different. He kept information. He wrote things down on small slips of paper torn out of notebooks or matchbooks. We would come across them all the time, cryptic notes like a napkin that said *20% of GNP* or *peanut futures/Japan*.

They piled up around the phone and on kitchen counters, pieces of ideas scratched on scraps of paper only he could decipher. Every now and then my mother would do a purge and sweep them all up into a manila folder, which she would then file somewhere in one of the many mysterious locking file cabinets in the house.

But just as he is losing everything else, nowadays Daddy has lost his hoarding instinct. It seems to have flipped over and become its opposite: a need to let things go, almost like a reaction to all those years of keeping, a late, great shucking off. The only things he seems intent on keeping now are his wallet, his glasses, the sheet of paper upon which I have written his name, age, and the names and ages of the rest of our family, and the napkin on which I have written *Alzheimer's disease.*

I often see him with his glasses on, bending over beneath a light, studying it.

chapter 16

My Infomercial

>———◦◦⊪◦◦）———

I nfomercials are both the insomniac's solace and their nightmare. At night, when I am not at the computer or calming
Daddy and talking him into going back to bed, I sink into their
manufactured world of paid audiences and 800 numbers. I float
away on the concepts of need and the fulfillment of need that
they provide. In the land of infomercials, all problems are solv-
able by things that can be paid for in easy installments of $39.95.
Contrary to their name, they bear no information worth having. Yet what the insomniac knows is this: They are better than
nothing. They are better than being alone late at night with
your runaway thoughts and fears.

Last night, when Daddy and Ava were sleeping, I actually
did it—I turned off the television.

In an instant my life came rushing at me. I am alone. My father is seriously losing it. He thinks I am his mother, or worse,
his wife. My baby stuffs crayons and Cheerios down her diapers.
Do all babies do this?

The roof is leaking in the studio, icicles the size of elephant tusks eclipse the view out the windows, providing the unique effect of being jailed by clear bars. What if the house collapses from the weight of all the snow? I have noticed that some of the beams in the basement are seriously rotted out—one side of the stone wall is bowed six inches from the foundation. Why didn't we see these things when we bought the house? I listen for the sound of crumpling wood, of beams giving way.

Fear breeds fear. Once you get going, God bless you. Say a prayer and hang on tight.

My worries are giants, they walk around with great clubs. I try to dodge their gargantuan feet. Fighting them off, I feel light-headed and dizzy.

What if Daddy gets out? What if he opens the wrong door and walks away into the night and disappears? What if I spend my whole life here and I raise Ava and see Daddy through to his grave and I get old and my life goes by and I am nothing but exhausted and used up and sad, and I never finish paying off the mortgage?

What if someone finds out how I feed Daddy and Ava hot dogs for days, forget to buy diapers and milk, and don't do the laundry, and they come and take her away from me? What if they say I am an unfit mother?

Or what if Ava grows up to hate me because I am so mad at Shane?

Don't get me started about Shane. In the televisionless night I close my eyes and picture him happy and dozing, in the arms of Marty, in an adobe house balanced on the tip of a red mesa beneath the North Star. A lucky place. The way I used to feel about my house. A place untainted by mind-robbing diseases, fear, or a baby's cries.

I have to be careful with my thoughts. If I'm not, hate fills me like a bottle. I am liquid anger. I am poison.

And so I whip the television back on and watch infomercials. I would rather watch people cook things in convection ovens than confront my life in the middle of the night. I would rather listen to Victoria Principal talk about her skin.

When I wake in the morning the baby is missing. My heart seizes. I leap from the bed and run into Daddy's room. He is gone, too. My fears have materialized. Could Daddy have gone outside—and taken Ava with him?

Taking the stairs in skips, I am calling to them: "Daddy! Ava!" What if she has no shoes on? Or drowns in the bathtub? I can smell my panic, an acid sweat. "Ava! Daddy!"

I run through the house half naked. Then I hear it. Po, the Teletubbie, Ava's talking toy. "Big hug. Ut-oh!"

I burst into the living room and there they are. Daddy and Ava, watching *Teletubbies* on the downstairs television and doing the Tubbie dance along with the little colored TV aliens.

"We're dancing," Daddy says. "Me and this little guy."

Daddy has his hands on his hips and is doing a sort of jig, and Ava is doing her favorite spin-around-until-you-fall-down dance.

"Isn't this something?" Daddy asks. "Come on, now, dance with us."

———◦✦✦◦———

I have become very good at pretending. I know how to make it seem like everything is normal, not letting on. I can do it. At work I just sit down and write, and everybody leaves me alone. They even gave me the Reporter of the Month award. For some reason they forgive me my eccentricities. Or maybe they just haven't noticed yet—my matted hair, my disheveled clothes.

At meetings, when it is my turn to talk, I just say a lot of words really fast so it seems like I have ideas. I can act pretty damn normal when I have to.

And now, with Jody Hackett hired, our home life is beginning to take on a semblance of normalcy. The mountains of laundry have begun to shrink. Ava hardly ever puts bottles in her ears anymore (largely because Jody has thrown away most of the bottles). And we have started to eat better, too, which is good, because Daddy looks like a famine victim.

Jody is Christian but she promises not to talk about Jesus with Daddy. She wants to help us, she says. She is worried about the old food rotting in the fridge, and though she doesn't say so, I can tell she is concerned about the mounds of unpaid bills. She teaches Ava to say "poo-ie" and hand me a diaper when she needs to be changed. Suddenly, within a month, Ava says "Thank you" and "No thank you." And "Bless you" when I sneeze.

Jody says she wants to help me find a good man. She has one. She recently married Dan Lasky, a state trooper. She feels bad that I am alone with Daddy and Ava. I think it goes against her deepest beliefs: that people should be in couples, that women who work hard should be rewarded with loving mates. With this in mind she introduces me to her friend Brian. Brian's ex-wife is manic-depressive and has left him alone with two young children. Jody invites him over to give us advice on re-doing our upstairs bathroom, a project she is undertaking with unflinching enthusiasm, like the rest of our lives. He stands in my house looking uncomfortable. He has on shoes with tassles. I hate shoes with tassles. We are polite to each other.

"I'm sorry," Jody says the next day. "I thought you might click."

"He's a nice man," I offer. "I can see why you are friends."

Jody makes Ava a little playroom out of a storage area. She fills it with pictures and toys. She organizes the kitchen and bathrooms. She looks for coupons in the paper and sales on baby shoes and tapes them to the refrigerator door.

But in spite of all her attention, in spite of clean clothes and scrubbed tubs, fresh fruit and dinners prepared from recipes she has clipped from *Gourmet* magazine (she subscribes), we get sick again, Daddy, Ava, and I. This time it is intestinal. Daddy shits in his pants. The way he describes it is "an implosion explosion."

Ava shits and pukes simultaneously. I hold her with one arm, the other arm bracing my own body, poised over the toilet as I puke. This goes on for thirty-five straight hours. We vomit after there is nothing left inside us. We heave air. We curl on the couch, waiting for spasms. Ava screams. Daddy groans.

I am thinking this must be as bad as life can get, but then I see the late-night news—there's a flood in Mozambique. People are waiting in trees to be rescued. There are not enough helicopters. They are standing atop the roofs of houses that are almost completely underwater, waving at cameras.

Daddy says, "Get me something clean, this shmata is disgusting." He smells.

It feels like all the energy I have is used to open the drawers, extract clean clothes for the three of us. I grab for a handful of diapers. When I come back, Daddy is puking again. Below him the cats are licking it up. I haven't fed them in days.

I can't help it. I yell at Shane. I yell at Mommy. Alone in my bedroom, I tell off people I haven't seen in years—roommates, ex-boyfriends, my sister. "Fuck you," I say.

The idea that they and their families are dry and warm and their stomachs settled makes me furious.

Then I call Dr. Eder, who says we must not get dehydrated. Ava and Daddy need constant infusions of water and Ava needs Pedialyte as well. I call Jody. "Help," I say.

"I have it, too," she says.

"At least we are not clinging to trees in Mozambique," I say.

"What?" she says.

Sometimes I think Jody suspects that I am losing it.

Then, suddenly, for two days in a row it turns to spring in late February: sixty-four degrees. We peel away layers of clothes. The freakish weather melts the snow, and we get well. We open the doors and breathe the warmer, new air. Above our house a wedge of geese barks down at us, as if heralding this sudden shift in temperature. We have soup and soda pop, not wanting to tempt fate with anything too heavy.

Then I decide on something. It is like a revelation, an epiphany: We should go somewhere. It seems like a completely novel idea.

My friend Elliot, who owns the health-food restaurant, likes Daddy. I appreciate the way he always talks to him as if he is normal; he focuses upon the things Daddy says that make sense.

Jody watches Ava so Elliot, Daddy, and I can go to hear Irish folk music at a café in Oxford, New York. In the car, Daddy and Elliot talk about the history of the American labor movement, the Wobblies, McCarthyism. "Crazy fiend," my father says.

"There are people whose lives were destroyed," Elliot says.

I shut my eyes and their conversation hums, like the tires, in the background. At the café we squeeze around a front table and order cups of steaming tea. Daddy looks around. "Hey, these women aren't half bad-looking here," he says to Elliot.

"Why do you think I come here?" Elliot replies with a wink.

The band is very young, and they play Irish reels and folk songs with a lilting accent. There are two brothers; one plays fiddle and the other, guitar. The vocalist is a beautiful girl who sways and stomps her feet as she sings. Daddy taps his feet and hums along, almost too loudly. All the way home he hums and sings to himself in the backseat. "Ah, the Irish," he says.

After we get back, Elliot calls me and says, "I still don't see what is so out of it about your father. He seems fine."

"Really? He does?"

"Sure, he seems normal, actually. The way you describe him I keep expecting someone really gonzo."

In a fit of ego and hope, I decide Daddy is improving. Living with me must be doing it. Something about me is restoring his memory. We were close when I was a child. We used to have a ritual called "midnight snack," which consisted of milk and cinnamon toast, eaten together after everyone else had gone to sleep. It was our secret, nobody else knew. We even washed up after ourselves, to remove the evidence. No wonder he is responding to me, I think, we have a special bond that has restorative qualities.

Furthermore, Daddy has remembered my name for two days running. When I asked him, he knew his favorite food—steak au poivre—and his most despised food—chicken. I decide to try and keep up the momentum, to try and go whole hog and cure him. Elliot helps. He tells me a story about how he could have cured a serious health disorder in his father if his dad would have just stuck with it. He says conventional medicine, with all its drugs and chemicals, just worsens many illnesses. "If I ever got cancer," he says, "I'd go the alternative route."

Elliot gives me a long list of vitamins, minerals, and foods to give Daddy. I stock up at a health-food store. I buy ginkgo root, garlic pills, carrots, and broccoli (antioxidants). I buy liver and castor oil. Fish. I put Daddy on a strict diet of memory food. Then I start to slowly begin the process of taking him off all his medications.

While I am shopping I see an AromaZone aromatherapy memory candle. The label says that "the essential oils of juniper and pettigrain are combined with a touch of basil to stimulate the intellect, relieve mental fatigue, and improve the memory."

Sounds good to me.

The candle makes me slightly queasy with its smoky herbal scent, but for Daddy the results of it—combined with all that memory-laden nutrition—appear immediate. He asks me one morning what I plan to write my column about that week.

"I don't know. I was thinking about tractors," I say. I want to write about all the old tractors in people's farmyards, how people never get rid of them, how they become like sculptures. I want to write about how people collect them, hoping someday they'll stumble across that one part they need for that old Cletrac, a brand that hasn't been manufactured since the 1950s. I will write about how they go on the Internet and talk to other tractor collectors.

Daddy says it sounds like a good idea for a column. "At least you know the farmers will like it," he says.

He asks me if we can have his famous chili for dinner. And here is the thing—he really does have a famous chili. At least it was famous among my mother, sister, and me. It is called "Daddy's famous chili" because it is the only thing he could ever really cook besides scrambled matzo-and-eggs. Whenever my mom needed a night off from cooking we would have matzo-and-eggs, SpaghettiOs, or Daddy's famous chili.

He even knows what we need to make it: kidney beans, hamburger meat, canned tomatoes, cumin, salt, pepper, chili pepper, and a dab of ketchup.

While we are eating the chili, Daddy bursts with wit and spontaneous humor. When Ava steals his fork, he calls her a "forklift." When she climbs onto the table and grabs the salt shaker, pouring white grains all over the floor, he says, "At least we know she's a mover and a shaker."

A frisson of success: I have done it. I am curing Alzheimer's disease.

I should make an infomercial.

I am washing the dishes late at night after everyone has gone to sleep, glowing with my success. I will cure Daddy, take a night-school class, and meet a new man (not an artist). We'll get married, fix the leaky part of the roof, shore up the basement, buy our own snowplow, and live happily ever after.

Daddy appears in the doorway. "I can't help it," he says. "I love you." He walks over behind where I stand, washing the plates, and puts his arms around me. "Kiss me," he says, and turns my head so that our lips touch hard.

"Daddy, don't. I am your daughter Beth. I am not Mommy."

"Oh, right."

He turns around slowly and leaves the room. I hear the sound of him shuffling upstairs. I feel a sense of muted panic rising in my throat. I know he didn't mean to upset me, that it is just "the disease talking," and I feel terrible for feeling so freaked out.

I finish the dishes and go upstairs to my room, where Ava is sleeping. I lie down beside her, wrapping my arms around her gently so as not to wake her. I let her little toes bury themselves beneath my leg.

For a long, long time I just lie there, listening to her breathe. I guess I didn't cure him after all.

chapter 17

Word Salad

That hand-wiping element = napkin
The chopped blocks = firewood
The soft cloth that I wipe around me = towel
The woman I love = Mommy
My mother = Mommy
That woman over there up north = Mommy
The protective mechanism = ashtray
The buckling item = belt
The dishing-up thingamajig = spoon
The place we go to where I hang my hat = home
That creature that makes all the noise = Samo
The little one = Ava
That little guy = Ava
That crying thing = Ava

Dr. Eder said word salad is the way Daddy and other people with Alzheimer's disease reach around to try and grasp at a concept that is no longer accessible to them. It is a compensation technique.

I begin to learn my father's word salad. I make a dictionary of his expressions; I call the list "Sanfordisms."

It is a bit like learning a new language; I am learning to speak Sanford, I tell Jody. She tells me she is learning it, too. Then she tells me she is learning to speak Ava, too, a far less mysterious language.

I feel bad because much of Ava's speech seems opaque to me. I experience that near-electrical surge of jealousy that I suppose many working mothers feel when they see their nannies have a special bond with their babies.

Jody shows me how Ava can identify her body parts. "Nose," she says. Ava points to her nose. "Ears." She points to her ears, then Jody's, and last of all mine. "Eyes." She points to her eyes and pinches those great, long lashes, just like her daddy's.

I was so wrapped up in this thing, the dilemma of us, I hadn't noticed Ava was learning so many words. She has entered the speaking world, with her own versions of "sit," "get up," "hungry," "go outside," "get me that," and "what's that?"

It takes concentration to decipher some of her phrases, but if you pay attention it is clear that her speech is a step up from baby talk. She is talking.

⇥————◄◦※◦◦►————

At first Daddy said he hated Jody. Now he is mellowing a little. Now he doesn't hate her, he just thinks she is a jerk.

Jody and Daddy fought over his cigarettes the other day. Jody would not give him one. He demanded; she refused. The way it works now is that people have to dole them out to him and then supervise his smoking.

Jody told him plainly that no, she would neither dole out nor supervise his smoking at that moment. She was changing a diaper. He stormed outside.

Later he told me, "I want you to fire that servant girl."

"We don't have a servant girl."

"That girl. The one who won't let me have a cigarette."

"That is Jody," I told him. "We need her to take care of the baby."

"What baby?" he asked.

"Ava."

"Oh, that little guy."

"It's a girl," I say.

Ava has her own word salad. "Duduninamadada," she tells me with authority. "Beekabeeka bebe Mommy and Pop-pop dosha."

Now that I am trying hard to translate, I think I know what the latter sentence means: "Baby shows Mama and Grandpa the cool dog over there." I am pretty confident I am right about this. I guess Jody would know for sure.

She points at her chest and says "baby." Then points at me and says "Mommy." She is very happy about this distinction.

Then she tells me a joke. "Baby," she says, pointing at my chest. "Mommy," she says, and she points at herself. She laughs and laughs.

She has a prefix she has begun to attach to many utterances: "beekabeeka."

Baby is "beekabeeka baby." Mama is "beekabeeka Mommy."

Life for Ava is very beekabeeka right now. She kisses her reflection in the mirror every morning, leaving little lip smudges behind. She kisses her shadow, she kisses her shoes. "Mine shoes," she says.

While for Ava, life is a grand adventure, full of whimsy and fun, Daddy and I aren't doing so well. I can't sleep at all. I fight the closing-eyelid syndrome on the long drive to work every morning. The other night I briefly considered calling a dial-a-psychic.

My father makes it clear he has grown weary of life. No beekabeeka for him. He is the very definition of existentialism.

To the question "Do you want butter or cream cheese on your bagel?" he answers, "What difference does it make?"

"You know," he says to me as I zip up his jacket, "you are not bad-looking."

"Thanks," I say.

"You want to hear something?" he asks.

I am not sure I do.

"I don't enjoy the work in Cleveland in the mines. It is taxing and I am not a young duck anymore," he says. "I am wasting my life away."

"Daddy," I say, "we are not in Cleveland. You haven't lived in Cleveland for fifty years. To my knowledge you have never been a miner."

"Then what is this mishegoss in my head? Tell me! What is this?"

"It's Alzheimer's," I say. "It's a disease in your brain."

"Damn that," he answers. "My memory may have a few little problems, but it's not that bad!"

I am exasperated by his denial. "If it isn't bad, then tell me," I say, "who am I?" I am being cruel.

"I know! I know who you are. You are that woman approximately one level down from me."

"As in daughter?"

"Right!"

Ava walks over to us and holds up her hands. "I think he wants some ice cream," Daddy says.

"Oh really?" It bothers me to think he, like Jody, understands Ava better than I do.

The baby walks over expectantly. She points at the freezer, where a quart of newly bought chocolate chip resides. She was there when we bought it and when I put it away. She remembers.

I dish out some for each of them. While I do, Ava sings us one of her little songs. "Mibamiba, mami miba dochado," she warbles. "Beekabeeka docha."

"Isn't that great?" asks Daddy. "He is singing about the dog!"

·——⊰⊙⊱——·

We have received our United States Census. Daddy is excited. "This is important," he says, waving it in the air.

I leave it on the desk and find him poring over it frequently, apparently reading the questions with the new glasses Jody bought him. We got the long form—fifty-three questions. They want to know how far I drive, my income, if we have electricity. They want to know about our toilets. I half expect them to ask if Ava is potty-trained yet.

"I guess I am here—person number two," Daddy says.

"Right," I say.

"And you, you must be person number one."

While I am at work he fills it in, chicken scratch writing, almost illegible. He gets his age—eighty—right, only he has written it in the space for our address. For his year of birth he writes *1973*.

And then he asks me his name.

"I can't remember. It is right on the tip of my tongue. Oh my God, it's getting really bad, isn't it? Am I getting worse, this Alzenheimer's?"

Sometime during the day, person three accomplishes two things. The first is that she discovers her own identity. "Aba!"

she declares, looking at her reflection in the full-length mirror in my bedroom. "Me! Aba!"

Her second accomplishment happens after I go to work. Somehow she gets her hands on the census. She crayons all over it, opening each page. Black Crayola in loopy thick scrawl that veers off here and there onto the dining room table.

"I don't know when she got it," Jody apologized. "I was barely out of the room for a minute."

But that was just the beginning of the wholesale destruction of our census. While I was washing dishes, Samo got ahold of it and chewed a big whole in the top.

I go to work and write my column about the census; about Persons No. 1, 2 and 3, and Household Pet No. 1. I tell the good people of Broome County how my daughter colored on the census and then the dog chewed it up. And how I realized that if I sent it in that way, scribbled and chewed, with Daddy's scrawled, confused responses beneath it all, it would say more about our family than the actual answers ever could.

———⋘∞⋙———

In the morning, Daddy gives me a big scare. "Come here, right now!" he yells urgently. I am getting dressed; he said he would finish feeding Ava her cereal. When I left them she was firmly strapped in her high chair and he was spooning oatmeal into her mouth. How could I leave her alone with him? Am I nuts?

"Hurry!" Daddy yells. I race downstairs in my bathrobe.

There they are, standing in the kitchen. There is no blood. There is no broken glass. Nobody is crying or unconscious. "What is it?" I ask.

"Watch," Daddy says.

Ava, standing in the middle of the room still wearing her bib, looks at him expectantly, awaiting her cue.

"Floor," Daddy says.

"Flo," says Ava, and crouches over, slamming her palms on the floor.

"How about that!" Daddy says. "I gave him a word!"

chapter 18

Things, and the Absence of Things

Along with my father have come a bunch of boxes. In a frenzied moment of organization, my mother had them sent to us. For a long time they remained in the middle of the living room, unopened. But bit by bit I have been venturing inside them, pulling out a few things a day and trying to find places for them in our lives.

Mostly they contain books. Some I remember from the shelves of the libraries in the houses where I grew up. They always symbolized for me the great intellectual substance of my parents' minds. Most of them are books I have never read. They are those books of the forties and fifties: small, condensed type; ragged-edged paper; sturdy, hard covers; and a feeling of real heft. These are books that say things. Their covers are usually one color. Their titles are placed simply, at the top, the author's name at the bottom. Books like Bruce Catton's *Terrible Swift Sword;* two-volume sets of the memoirs of General William Tecumseh Sherman and Harry Truman; a three-volume set of William Hickling Prescott's *History of the Conquest of Mexico;* Max Lerner's *America As a Civilization* and two volumes of Oswald Spengler's *The Decline of the West;* Marcel Proust's *Remembrance of Things Past; The Rise and Fall of the Third Reich,* by William Shirer; John Rae's *Contemporary Socialism.*

These are the books that had given rise to my brief fantasy that my parents were once communists, that I was an exotic red-diaper baby. I had asked my dad about it over dinner at a particularly volatile time in my adolescence when I reveled in my ability to shock. We'd had people over for supper from the economics department, and as my mother served slices of her homemade strawberry-glazed cheesecake, I'd casually asked, "So what was it like in the Communist Party when you guys were young?"

My dad, never willing to let me one-up him, turned with equal casualness and replied: "Boring. Their meetings were so boring. I couldn't tolerate them."

The rest of the books in the boxes are probably classics in his field of labor economics. They have many charts and graphs inside, and terribly dull titles like *Wage and Salary Administration* and *The General Theory of Employment, Interest, and Money.* I page through a few of them, thinking I might gain some insight into my father's past. Glover and Cornell's *The Development of American Industries,* written in 1941, is of no help whatsoever.

But in some, like *The Common Law of the Workplace,* I find essays by people I knew to have been my parents' friends, like Gladys Gershenfeld. I met her once. She was an arbitrator like Daddy. She and her husband had numerous brilliant sons, who went to schools like MIT and Harvard. One was the subject of a recent article in *Time* magazine on geniuses.

In a few books and journals, I come upon essays by my father. Some journals contain published copies of his arbitration decisions. Some books he helped edit, like *Management Preparation for Collective Bargaining*. And there is book after book with only his name on his spine: *Labor Law* and his famous *Labor in the United States, Volumes I, II, III, IV, and V.* It seems that after a while my father had taken to writing the same book, over and over again. I opened *Volume V* the other day, turned to a random page and read: "An important implication that can be drawn from the analysis of demand under oligopolistic conditions is that a policy of price stability by the seller makes a good deal of sense."

While I was reading, my father came into the room. "That book, let me see that."

I showed him the spine. "That book is mine," he said. "I wrote it."

"You did, Daddy," I said.

Reading the words he once wrote reveals why his speech can be so hard to understand. He still peppers it with the same pedantic words he always used. In the course of a day, words like *analysis, politics, economics, labor, stability,* and *university* work their way into his conversations. Although I have repeatedly told him I am a journalist and work at a newspaper, when I leave each morning he asks me if I am "off to the university." When he talks about the future he always says "next semester." These words are a part of him. They do not desert him, even at this time when so many other things do. A shell of language remains, like a hard casing his mind has left.

In the boxes are other things, too. Tchotchkes, like a ceramic mask from Mexico; pots, menorahs, three antique statues of saints. My parents were very eclectic. They liked the accoutrements of Judaism—the customs, the lingo, the history. The actual beliefs they eschewed. We always had Passover Seders, but they were not spiritual events, they were about food. My mother was a very good cook.

In the boxes, I see she has sent me some of her cookbooks. She has not cooked in several years. When I see them, I realize that she never intends to cook again. She is passing on the act of cooking to me. Her books are annotated with little suggestions to herself—like *This is good with poppy seeds, too* and *Add a squeeze of lemon for some punch* and *Use the high-altitude version.* This is sort of sad, since I am known in my family as an abysmal cook. I will never add poppy seeds to the "plain yellow cake" in *The Molly Goldberg Jewish Cookbook,* nor a squeeze of lemon to the Milanese chicken recipe she has cut out of a magazine and pressed between the pages of *The Joy of Cooking.*

In the boxes there is also a leather belt with a beautiful silver and turquoise buckle, and a silver box from Thailand that has an elaborate casing and a mahogany interior with an engraved silver plaque. It says: *To Dr. Sanford Cohen in deep appreciation from the Organizing Committee Southeast Asian Seminar on Manpower Development and Educational Planning.*

Manpower. That is another word Daddy often uses. One morning he said we needed to get some more manpower in my house. I think he meant we need to hire a cleaning lady.

When I ask him about the Thai box, who it was from and where and when he got it, he looks at me blankly. "It looks so familiar, but I just can't get at it," he says sadly, shaking his head.

We may have a lot of boxes in our lives now, but stuff is

missing, too. Mostly CDs. Shane didn't take much, but what he took seems to pockmark the house with need. I miss Tom Waits. I miss Natalie Merchant. I miss certain shirts we sort of shared, and maybe I am crazy, but I couldn't find my toothbrush right after he left.

I can never tell if things are missing because Shane took them to Gallup or because they were just moved somewhere by Daddy. It is unsettling the way people must feel after their homes have been robbed and they are trying to establish what exactly is gone.

I tried to box up some of Shane's stuff after he left but aborted the project because it was too depressing and seemed like a favor to him at a time when I didn't feel like doing him favors. I had briefly entertained the idea of sending several gigantic boxes C.O.D. to Marty's house. But I left the first box open and half packed in the living room, where it continues to sit, a gaping mouth that chides my weakness as I trip across it at night when I go to the bathroom.

I can't help it. I read more of Shane's e-mails from Marty. I can tell they had slept together. They already had secrets. In her e-mails she alludes to things in that intimate code that lovers have. They share secrets and jokes. I try to remember if I had any secrets or private jokes with Shane. I can't come up with any.

Ava gets boxes in the mail, too. All my friends who have had children late in life and don't plan on any more send me their kid stuff. Candelora Versace, in Santa Fe, sends spectacular outfits. Purple velvet overalls, petite dresses, and jackets in deep-red corduroy. Other friends send me tiny sweats and sneakers, T-shirts and toys. Lots of toys. Things that stack and talk and float in the bathtub. People spend a lot on their first children.

Ava has memorized all her toys and made them citizens in her country, the land of Ava. And with the help of Jody—a firm believer in the importance of baptism—she has named them. She calls a black-and-white stuffed leopard "Stucco." She calls a small pink stuffed dachsund "Ruff." The plastic dump truck is "Trucky." A plastic rocking horse is "Gooboy." She always pats its head and says, "Gooboy, Gooboy" and sometimes "Down-boy." One day I realized, she speaks to it just the way I do to Samo, our dog. She is saying "Good boy, good boy," and, like I do, "Down, boy."

I get boxes, too. My friends feel sorry for me. When they call, they can tell I am exhausted. I have admitted to most that Shane has left. The whole situation eventually got reported throughout the network of gossip, even though I have sworn to myself that I will not whine.

But my friends are good friends. They want to make me feel better, and I have to admit it—bald-faced materialist that I am—they do. From Jenny Lyn Bader I get packages from Balducci's in lower Manhattan. Smoked salmon and crackers and cheeses and chocolate. From David Margolick I get books of poems, antique postcards of New Mexico, and clipped articles from *The New York Observer* and *The Jerusalem Report* on topics he must think interest me.

From Sandy Garritano in San Francisco, I am overnighted fresh strawberries and blueberries, cheeses, and all sorts of vegetables. She sends me vitamins and everything necessary to make her favorite vegetable soup, even a pot. It comes all the way to Beartown Road without even so much as a sign of wilt or a brown spot. The night the packages arrive, I sit on the icy front porch, after Daddy and Ava are asleep, and I eat a bowl of fresh blueberries and cream.

Sandy also sends me boxes and boxes full of gorgeous clothes with matching silk scarves and jewelry. She bought them to go to conferences with her brain surgeon husband in Europe and Japan and never wore them. Now I wear them in this house where a brain disintegrates.

Sometimes I wish I could take Daddy to a place where doctors and scientists would study him. On Daddy's driver's license, issued in 1996, he checked the box that asks if you wish to donate your body to science. Maybe Daddy could help them make sense of this disease. Maybe he would want that. I do not know.

All the things—Daddy's, Ava's, and mine—and boxes are piling up. I never seem to have the energy to put anything away. We make little paths around and through them, to the bathroom, dining room, and stairway. We get sort of used to them.

There are other new things around, too. Ever since I enrolled Daddy in the GROW program, he has been making things. GROW meets in a church.

"It's a church," Daddy says each time we pull up.

"It is just *in* a church, it isn't religious."

"Then why in a church?" he asks.

"They have to have it somewhere," I say.

In adult day care they play bingo. They sing, they do exercises and eat lunch. They go through the newspaper together. And they make things. Daddy has made a refrigerator magnet out of a clothespin, with pink cotton balls glued to it so it resembles a pink caterpillar. It even has glued-on plastic eyes. He glued blue star buttons onto a tiny straw hat, and on Easter he dyed an egg. Daddy wins bingo. He brings home a tiny basket full of bath salts and lotion, which he says he wants to give to his mother.

I cringe when I see the clothespin caterpillar, with its plastic eyes that jiggle. A smiling face with cotton-ball cheeks. These things he makes are beneath him. Can't they see that? He should be listening to classical music or seeing slide shows of someone's trip to China.

If he has to make anything, why can't it be something less juvenile? Why can't they honor his dignity? He tells me, "I hate that class. It is like third grade. What did I do to deserve this?"

"Daddy, just grit your teeth, Dr. Eder says it is good for you."

"Please, don't make me go," he begs.

"Just go a couple more times, Daddy," I say.

"How much are they paying me to teach those dummies?"

When he says this I realize he thinks he is the teacher. He thinks he is teaching a class of idiots. He would flip if he knew I pay them for him to go.

That is when I do it: I lie.

"A small stipend," I say. "Nothing much, just a little check, but it helps out around here."

"How come I never see the check?"

"I put it right in the bank, Daddy, with all your other money."

"Everyone is always telling me I have all this money, but I never see any of it." He turns his pockets inside out. "Look, I am penniless."

• • •

Late at night I hear noises and rise, thinking he is down there, rearranging things again. I throw on a robe and go downstairs to see what is going on, but I can't find him. I catch my breath when I see that the door to Shane's studio is ajar. I keep it closed all the time. Inside I see Daddy. He has forded the stream of chewed papers and debris and gone farther, into the cavernous painting room. He has switched on the lights, and when I walk in he is standing there in the freezing room, in his pajamas, looking around in awe. "Look what I found!" he says. "It's wonderful. Look at the colors."

He walks from painting to painting, running his hands over the canvases thick with images. "It is a treasure trove." He spins toward me and holds his hands out in an expression of wonder. "Did you know all this was down here?"

"I knew, Daddy."

"Just look, look at these faces!"

Shane paints faces. He paints red hills and figures that seem lost among them. He paints the skyscrapers of New York City and tiny people on the streets below. Some of our fights were about the fact that he often painted to the exclusion of all else. Most housework, child care, pet care, shopping, bill-paying, and appointment-making were left up to me.

My father walks over to a small painting of Gallup and picks it up. "I have the sense I have seen this before. Do I own this one?"

"No, Daddy," I say. "But maybe you recognize it. You used to live near there, in Albuquerque."

Once, when I lived in Gallup, Daddy drove out to see me. He drove all the way to my house, a little apartment at the edge of a mesa, following directions and getting lost only once. He made it right to my door. We had a good time together. He came with me to a remote restaurant about which I had to write a review. We sat at a table by a window and looked out at the sky and hills. It was 1996. I had just met Shane and I was in love. I had no idea that it was miraculous, Daddy's visit. That it may have been the last solo trip of his life. I was caught up in my own situation, blinded to his. It might have been the last time we ever spent together with all his pistons firing properly. Thinking back, I had found him a bit odd. He misplaced things in my house. He could not remember his phone number in Albuquerque. But it had not seemed important. He was getting on in years, after all.

He was still Daddy then, the absentminded professor. I should have appreciated him more.

In a way, the cluttered effect of our house now is a good thing. Whenever I start to think our lives suck, I have to step over a box and remember that life is going on here. We make messes, therefore we are. Normal people have problems with clutter. You can read about it in women's magazines. It makes us a part of the vast republic of the messy. Right now being a part of any society is something I'll take. It is better than feeling all alone and crazy in a universe of three.

Jody and I are keeping my father busy and active, and there are people out there who care about us. I no longer have to dig through piles of dirty clothes to get dressed. Because of Sandy's packages I have outfits. I look put together. It is the nature of the American office that people notice these things. It makes me feel better when I get up, just knowing I look like a regular person going to work. Even if I am faking it.

As for Daddy and Ava, they are both delighted by all the new things, the things that arrive in boxes. Daddy took a volume of *Labor in the United States* with him to the dining table the other night and just sat there, turning it over and over, staring at it like it was the most marvelous thing in the world.

Ava, of course, thinks the things Daddy makes at adult day care are for her. She cries when I take them away to put in a drawer in Daddy's bedroom, but I have to. A lot of them have pieces that could be swallowed.

Meanwhile, she revels in the boxes themselves. She gets inside them and plays peekaboo and obscure games that involve, strangely, plastic blocks full of water she dishes out of the cat bowls and inevitably spills. Sometimes she pushes a chair to the sink and fills her big Legos with water. It makes Daddy nervous, so I follow behind her, mopping up. Ava looks so big now. Jody says she is far beyond her years in development (something all mothers thrill to hear; I have noticed that everyone's babies are "far beyond their years" in at least one area). Ever a hoarder, she fills the boxes with blocks and Cheerios, little books, dolls, and the cups of water. I can hear her inside, talking to them.

In the bathroom my father is shaving. He is humming a song. It makes me happy that he can still do this, shave and be happy. The people at adult day care think he should be supervised at all times, but I still let him shave and shower alone. He may do a sloppy job, but he seems to need the ritual, this last vestige of an independent adult life.

He is talking, too. Or saying the words to a song. I can't hear what either Ava or Daddy is saying in their private worlds—she in the box, he in the bathroom—but in both cases it seems a happy sound, not unlike what you might hear in a normal family in a normal house where boxes are emptied and things are organized in closets and drawers.

I write a column called "The Importance of Being Normal." Then I throw it away.

chapter 19

A Miracle Passes

Yet another storm hits us hard. It is particularly depressing because a few freak days of warm weather had given us a break, made us hopeful. It is mid-March, and we are ready to say good-bye to this winter, but now we are assaulted by a full-blown blizzard. The snow is very wet and thick, and as usual the plows have pushed it to the sides of the road in icy mounds higher than the car. I cannot get out of the driveway.

This time nobody comes to plow us out. I go outside with a shovel and dig at the ice for a while until I am covered in sweat. I have made little progress on the five-foot tower blocking the drive. Finally I manage to carve a small dent in the wall and then try to knock the rest over with the car in four-wheel-drive reverse. It doesn't work. The car spins and whines and spits ice into the air.

Snow is becoming the theme of our lives, our leitmotif. It underscores the truth of us, that we are isolated in our situation. Snow is very sneaky. The flakes gently envelop the yard, all the while looking so beautiful. And then suddenly it whispers, "You are stuck."

Snow cuts us off. It falls and falls and then makes icy fences we cannot escape.

I finally give up and go back inside. But it is lonely in there with the two of them. Strangely, Daddy and Ava seem to be able to communicate just fine—they jabber back and forth to themselves and each other. I alone am left with nobody to talk to. Talk as in really *talk*. Not baby talk. Not Daddy's in-and-out-of-reality banter. I ask Daddy if he wants to do our memory project and he says no. He says he can't "remember any memories" today.

The snow begins to swallow the house; fat flakes fall and wind pushes them against the windows, which are steamy and fogged. We lose our telephone service and then our electricity. I light a few candles, and then Daddy and I start up fires in the woodstove and the fireplace, and they heat the house. The woodstove really cranks, but we have to keep foraging out to the woodpile, and the woodpile is getting harder and harder to find. Each time we bring in loads of wood they are wetter and icier than before. We have to prop them by the fireplace or put them atop the stove to dry out before we throw them in the fire or they sputter and spit and refuse to ignite. Whenever I place a newly retrieved log in the stove it sizzles and sends up a plume of steam. Tiny melted snow drops dance on top of the burner.

When Daddy goes for wood he always comes back with a single log, and each time he says the same thing: "This ought to keep us warm all night."

Each time a log turns orange-bright and begins to move toward ash, I have to ask him to go out again. I am afraid to leave

Ava alone and get wood myself. She has a temperature again. I think it is just from teething, but I am not sure.

I touch Daddy's shoulder. "The fire is getting low again."

He puts on gloves and a coat, hat and scarf, to go out for wood. He doesn't come back. Minutes go by. I open the door and call for him. No answer. Ava is pulling on her left ear incessantly. I don't want to leave her wailing in the crib but think maybe I'll have to. I move from window to window, peering through white in the dark. Evening is approaching.

Finally I hear a pounding on the back of the house, the laundry room window. I rush back there and see him, flushed and red from the cold, frightened-looking. I wave him around the side of the house. "Daddy, over here, over here!" I yell.

He stumbles onto the porch, soaked to the skin. Snow is down his coat, in his boots; he is freezing. "I had quite a scare," he said. "I lost my perspective on my orientation to my bearings in space."

He shivers while I peel off his wet layers and move him in front of the woodstove to warm up. "The woodpile is right over there, to the left of the house, Daddy."

"I know that, I know that. But when you get out there it is just white all over; left and right don't matter anymore."

From then on I put Ava in her crib and go out for the wood myself. Each time, she cries hard, like I am leaving her for good in an orphanage. Each time, I feel like a traitor when I walk out of her room, where she stands and clings to the sides of the crib, strands of sweat-soaked hair stuck to her face. She sobs. "No go, Mommy."

"I'll be right back, honey, I am just going out to get some wood."

"Take Ava!" she screams.

Being left is her weakness. She hates any good-bye. Even if I am just going to the bathroom, she latches on to me. "Take Ava," she orders.

But I have to leave her to keep us warm. We have gotten through so many storms, I know we'll weather this one, too. I am getting to be an old pro. I used to depend on Shane to make fires. We neatly split all chores down gender lines: me dishes, him trash; me cooking, him cat litter changes. In the world of the male and female division of labor, fires are clearly in the realm of men. Now I am sure I am better at it than he is.

I used to depend on him for a lot of things. I remember how he had made a fire the year before, when we first bought the house. We hadn't bought any wood, and he went outside and collected pieces of old fallen trees, branches, used handfuls of the tiny pinecones from the trees in the front yard for kindling. I had thought him so resourceful. But I have redefined resourceful, taken it to another level now. Every week I bring home stacks of old newspapers from the office. One night I burned an old broom. It ignited as fast as gasoline and sent a whirl of sparks shooting up the chimney. When the flame calmed it left behind a perfect broom-shaped skeleton of ash.

Wouldn't Shane be impressed by me? I take care of us. His daughter. Doesn't he wonder how his daughter is? I think, maybe tonight will be the night he calls.

But it won't be. The phone goes dead for the second time— and stays dead. This time I get claustrophobic. I start to talk to myself: "Now, don't get weird on me," I tell myself. "Just three more logs until morning."

I am afraid to go to sleep, because the fire might go out and

I am not sure I can get it going again. The wood is pretty wet. For a while I actually put logs in the oven to dry them out, which worked pretty well. But when the electricity went out I was left without that option.

As the sun rises there is a knock on the door. It is Mr. Wright. I'm sure he is coming to check in on us, see how we weathered the storm. During the last storm he brought us hurricane lamps and oil.

But when I open the door he looks upset. Recently his wife, Betty, told me he is ill. "He has the Parkinson's," she said. "See how he shakes?"

They told me that because of his Parkinson's, they are thinking they might put their place up for sale. It is quite a place: 160 acres, a huge barn, a house, an in-ground pool, two ponds, and meticulous grounds. Mr. Wright keeps every inch of it pristine. Another neighbor once told me that if a leaf falls somewhere on Mr. Wright's property, he knows about it. Having Parkinson's must scare him.

He bursts in, careful to stomp his boots on the mat until every fleck of snow has fallen off them. It leaves snowy imprints in the shapes of his boot treads. "I would've plowed you out there and shoveled your walk but we had a real bad accident. Little Danielle." I realize that his eyes aren't tearing from the cold and wind. He is crying. Crying real tears. I am so happy to see him—another person with whom I can actually speak, who can perhaps even help me bring in a load of wood. But seeing Mr. Wright crying destroys that feeling of being rescued. Instead it contributes to the sense that life is spinning out of control like the swirling snowflakes in the hard wind.

"What happened?"

"Her arm, it got all caught up in the tractor. Mark was plowing out, he was going to pull the sled, and it got caught in there."

Danielle is the eldest of Mr. Wright's five grandchildren and the apple of his eye.

"She would have bled to death except for her jacket. The hospital people said that jacket saved her, it got twisted up and somehow worked like a tourniquet. Thank goodness Mark didn't try to take it off, he just grabbed her up and drove to the hospital with her in his arms on his lap, just drove right in, as fast as he could go."

He tells us that Guthrie One—the emergency chopper—was unable to fly in the storm, so they were not able to take her down to the bigger hospitals in Sayre, Pennsylvania, or up to Syracuse. The less-experienced doctors at Wilson Memorial Regional Medical Center had to try to reattach her arm.

"Oh, Mr. Wright." I move to hug him. He waves me away, holding his hand to his face.

"I am driving Betty down there now, we're gonna spend the day down there, we just want to know if she's all right. It's touch and go."

He turns and leaves, the door slamming behind him. As he does, a gust of snow flutters into the living room.

"So, so, so," Ava says, reaching for the flakes.

"Good God," my father says.

By Tuesday the county snowplows have cleared the roads and our other neighbors have shoveled out the car. Someone, in either a fit of pity or Christianity, left a plastic container full of biscuits on our doorstep. They are cold and hard as rocks, covered in neat flowered paper napkins. I look around as though I might catch a glimpse of the baker-philanthropist hiding in the brush. People are kind.

Jody makes it over and I drive to work. When I get there I say, "I have a news story for you. A little girl may have lost her arm up in Colesville." I say I can't write the piece myself, I know the family. Linda Jump, the Delaware County reporter, writes it. But when I sit down to write my column I can't help it. I write about Danielle's arm. Her arm suddenly seems like the only thing in the world that matters.

Apparently, a whole chain of people all across the country hear about Danielle over the Internet and are praying for her. At the eleventh hour it looks like the arm might be saved, a miracle really, since it was terribly mangled in the tractor, caught up in the power start.

The paper follows Danielle's fate play-by-play, and the whole community holds its breath. Daddy, so oblivious to everything recently, is right in there with them. He keeps asking, "How is that little girl's arm?" and "Any word yet on the arm situation?"

But the miracle passes. The arm does not take. It is amputated later that afternoon, a few days after the accident. When I tell Daddy, he collapses onto the sofa. "What a shame, what a waste, what a tragedy," he says, wiping away tears. He cries a lot now.

The day after Linda Jump's article runs, the letters pour in. People send checks, they want to know how they can help. They start holding benefits for Danielle. The first one—a spaghetti dinner at Brother's Two restaurant in the adjacent town of Endwell—attracts more than a thousand people. They each pay ten dollars to get in, but all through the evening I see people walk up to the organizers with envelopes and hand them over.

In all, more than forty thousand dollars is raised for Danielle. I tell Daddy.

"That's a lot of money," he says. "But it isn't an arm."

chapter 20

Ersatz Life

"You want to hear a memory? I'll give you a memory: Yalowitz's Delicatessen. In Cleveland. Best damn pastrami sandwich around. Corn beef could knock your socks off."

My father is showing me he can remember. We write it down. It is his job, he says. We try to write down a memory a day now. "For posterity."

"Here in this ersatz life, this quasi-death, it gives us a sense of purpose," he says.

"Right, Dad."

He waxes poetic about the pastrami. "And the rye bread. Did they have a rye bread!"

My father asks me if I ever knew his mother.

"No, Daddy, I was just a baby when she died."

Her name was Celia. Daddy's father was Louis. His Hebrew name was Shlomo. "He worked hard as a plasterer," Daddy says. "My mother stayed home and did people's laundry. They had only one wish for me in life, that I should work indoors."

My father tells me they were upset when he didn't want to

go and work for my Uncle Harry, a butcher. Then asks me, "Did you write all that down?"

"Yes," I say.

"Where?"

"Here. Yalowitz's."

"I think it's Yalowitz's with a *c*."

"Where is the *c*?"

"Somewhere at the end there."

"Yalowictz's?"

"Something like that."

After telling me about the deli, Daddy tells me about his hands. Apparently, when he was a little boy, he had a terrible rash for several consecutive summers. Tiny itchy blisters covered his skin, and they would pop and become running sores. "My mother had to keep putting on salve and wrapping me up. I was wrapped up to here," he says, pointing to his forearm. "I couldn't play, I couldn't write, I couldn't do anything!"

"What was it?"

"What?"

"The rash, what was it from?"

"Oh, poison ivy or something. I never knew."

I wonder what it is that makes him remember the rash. I think it might be Ava; she has discovered Band-Aids. She knows I keep them under the sink. Although I have told her not to, whenever I look away for a moment, she gets them and takes them to Daddy. "Put on Ava," she says. She wants them on her knees, her chin, and her hands. It is partly my fault. I bought some sort of Disney-themed brand. They even glow in the dark.

· · ·

The weather has turned wet and sticky. It is April, and with the cold retreating I am again trying to improve our lives. I get tickets to a Neil Simon play and to a 1950s musical revue called *Radio Days.* Dr. Connor said I am supposed to keep us busy, do lots of things. That is supposed to help Daddy stave off depression.

It could help me, too, I think. Staying home is exhausting. The phone stares at me. Even though I have purged it, the house still speaks of Shane. Certain walls where his paintings were retain their outlines in dust. Occasionally I find things, a single slipper, a paintbrush—rock-hard and blue—a paint-stained T-shirt.

The house gets so messy that I spend all my time putting things away, cleaning up. That is when I find the things.

I choose a play as a diversion. A movie would be easier, but Daddy doesn't understand movies anymore. I tried to take him and Ava one weekend and it was a disaster. I put him in a row near the exit to watch *The Cider House Rules,* then I took Ava across the hall to see *The Tigger Movie.* Ava watched about twelve minutes before she got restless and started kicking the seat in front of her. "Ava go home bye-bye!" she said aloud. "Now, Mommy."

She is not ready for movies.

At the exact moment when we walked out of *The Tigger Movie,* Daddy was exiting *The Cider House Rules.*

"That was the most ridiculous movie," he said. "It was just terrible. Made no sense at all."

He is past movies. That time for him is gone.

But for the Neil Simon play, Daddy gets excited. He has always loved theater. The night of the play, Jody watches Ava. Daddy and I eat sandwiches so we don't get too messy. He has put on a nice suit and tie. I notice that the pants are the pants that once went with his tux. Black pants with a stripe of black silk down the side. "How's that for a handsome guy?" he asks.

In the car, on the way, he puts his hand on my arm. "Do you love me?" he asks.

"Of course I do."

"Can I make love to you?"

I catch my breath. The car swerves into the next lane. A blue pickup honks and its driver flips me off.

"Daddy," I say, "that would be weird. You're my father."

Silence.

"I am?"

"Yes."

"I don't feel like anybody's father," he says.

Daddy loves the Neil Simon play. Light and fast-paced, it is about a party in Manhattan where someone gets shot—not fatally—and a bunch of people try to cover it up. He laughs and laughs. "This is very good, I'm impressed," he says.

He looks around at the audience during intermission. It is a full house. Daddy had predicted nobody would come, since it is pouring rain. "Who are all these people?" he asks, as if I could tell him their names, one by one.

"I don't know, Daddy," I say. "I'm pretty new in this town."

"They all came out in this bad weather," he says.

"They did," I say.

I tell my sister about what Daddy said to me in the car. "It's sort of creepy," I say.

"Oh, deal," Melanie says. "It's just the Alzheimer's."

"I know that," I say. I tell her how I try to say "Daddy" every time I address him, to orient him to me as a daughter.

"Well, that's pretty stupid," she says. "That's what Mommy calls him, too."

She is right. It is. How could I have forgotten that?

Daddy remembers the play for days. Keeps talking about it. He even remembers the name of the theater: the Cider Mill Playhouse. "That was really very funny," he says. I wonder if he remembers what he said to me on the way there, as well. Then I change the subject in my mind.

I don't want to think about my father in the car. So I think about funny. What is funny? Ava thinks it is funny to pull the cats' tails. She thinks it is funny to blow bubbles in the bathtub. She can say "bubbles." She can say "bath." Sometimes she even says "bubble bath."

She thinks it is funny when I say, "Ava, throw the ball at the bubbles in the bath!"

She cracks up. Her laughter is deep, real, convulsive. Sometimes her laughs turn into crying. I think of laughter as part of a circle of emotion that ends up as sadness if you go far enough. My job is to keep her centered in the laughter. Daddy, too. He laughs a lot, but he has also begun to sob uncontrollably, numerous times a day.

I call Dr. Eder. "What should I do?" I ask. "He's crying all the time."

Dr. Eder calls in a prescription for Prozac to the pharmacy. He is to take one pill before sleep at night. "It takes a couple weeks to kick in," Dr. Eder warns.

I give him his Prozac religiously with a glass of orange juice before bed each night. "Pill time," he says merrily when I dole out his meds.

Each day he takes Prozac; Aricept; the über-vitamin E (1,000 mg); Lipitor, a cholesterol-reducing drug; Adalat, a blood pressure med; and a baby aspirin. A fistful of pills. Sometimes I wonder what would happen if I stopped giving him the Lipitor and his blood vessels clogged up with cholesterol, and he had a heart attack and died.

He has expressed misery at life numerous times. The only thing he seems to regularly enjoy is eating. He likes steaks, lamb chops, sausages—high-cholesterol foods that don't seem to stick to his ribs at all. What if I fed him the things he loves around the clock, the foods that would bring about his natural death? It could put him out of his misery. Then I wouldn't have to answer his questions all day and night: "Where is my mother? What is she doing there? Where is he? Who am I? Whose baby is that?"

Every day he tells me how dull his life is, how unhappy he feels. If I fed him meat and withheld the Lipitor and he died, could I be accused of assisted suicide?

These are the sorts of thoughts I have been having.

Within a week and a half of starting him on the Prozac, Jody and I see a difference: Daddy begins to sing.

Interestingly, so does Ava. Their voices tip into song at the slightest provocation. They wail, they hum, they sing little ditties and deep, dark beautiful melodies. Ava—not knowing many words yet—sings in baby talk. Daddy sings oldies. Real oldies. He sings:

> "In Dublin's fair city
> where girls are so pretty
> 'twas there that I met her

sweet Molly Malone
She wheeled a wheelbarrow
through streets wide and narrow
singing "Cockels and mussels
alive, alive-o"
She died from the fever
And nothing could save her. . . ."

He forgets the rest. He says the song is haunting him. He hums and sings it constantly. He says it is the sound track to his dreams as well. Then he tells me there is another song he can't get rid of . . . but he can't quite remember it, either. He asks me to sing it to him.

"It goes, 'Suddenly, I'm not half the man I used to be . . .' "

My father begins to cry in a torrent. Wiping tears away on the backs of his hands, he says, "A shadow is hanging over me."

Ava sings along.

She sings with him in a wordless, musical language she invents, and the singing begins to be shouting and then it returns to singing. Then she, too, begins to cry, as if sensing Daddy's despair.

Her songs are often tiny, circuitous melodies that have no clear beginning or end. Most of them sound like the theme song to *Elmo's World* or they are like "Old McDonald Had a Farm" or "Twinkle, Twinkle, Little Star." Daddy remembers these songs and sings along with her. Certain songs—like "Row, Row, Row Your Boat"—have been around so long they have probably become encoded in human DNA by now.

Daddy knows all the words and the melody to "Twinkle, Twinkle, Little Star." He even stays on key. He and Ava can actually harmonize, in a way.

While Ava sings she often dances. She rocks from one leg to another, waving her arms, and then she twirls and twirls around. She is so tiny, and the twirling seems so sophisticated for her seventeen-month-old frame.

The other morning I left the two of them together in the gated-off living room while I took a shower. When I got out I saw Daddy had turned on the stereo, and they were dancing and singing with Al Green, the song "Love and Happiness," which I'd left in the CD player. I walked in and they both took my hands and started pulling me into the music. We all danced until Ava got so dizzy from spinning she collapsed, and Daddy and I fell down beside her, laughing. Ava climbed on top of each of us and gave us Eskimo kisses. Then she went around the room and kissed every toy. She kissed the cup, her bottle, the radio, her own foot. She kissed the doorknob. She kissed the cat.

She kissed me again and then her Pop-pop.

"He's so affectionate," Daddy said.

"Yes, Daddy," I said, overcome with affection for my beautiful Ava. "Yes, he is."

I must admit that, while the management of day-to-day affairs can seem impossible, things are sometimes pleasant. I think of our lives as something akin to the way that people in covered wagons might have felt. Exhausted, scared, but grateful for certain moments. We take pleasure in small things. Daddy likes the smell of coffee brewing. Ava likes to blow bubbles with her saliva while mouthing the word "Mama." I like to sit in the kitchen with the two of them, eating, cleaning up around them, feeling like I have a bit of control. That they are getting nourishment. That I am doing something right.

Interestingly, even though his memory is compromised, Daddy makes us touch the past every day. He *is* the past. With him here, time bends and buckles—2000 meets 1920, and vice versa. He tells me about his sister, Esther ("She was always my favorite") and brother, Sol, both of them much older.

"I might have been an accident," he says, and winks at me.

Compared to the past, the present is not interesting to him. He doesn't even watch the news now, although he and my mother watched it obsessively all their lives. The flood in Mozambique, the people in the trees; airplane crashes in which hundreds die; the coming election—it all seems to go right over him. The war in Chechnya, which would have elicited a vehement response years ago, inspires a yawn. The Pope's visit to Cuba seems to completely bore him; but most shocking, he seems indifferent to the idea that in Israel there is talk of giving the Palestinians some control over a part of Jerusalem. There was a time when that would have made him so mad he would have thrown something. Instead he smiles bemusedly. He is fixated on his past. Stuck. He tells me the same stories over and over.

"I have always been in pretty good health, just look at me," Daddy says. "But did I ever tell you that, when I was little, I had the worst rash on my hands every summer? My mother didn't know what to do with me. She'd wrap my hands in ointment and cloth, it was so uncomfortable! It ruined the summers."

I pretend he hasn't told me the story before. "What caused the rash?" I ask, as if I don't know that he doesn't know.

"Something in Cleveland," he says. "Poison ivy, I think."

"Really?" I say.

───◄◄H◄◄►───

I check out *How to Care for Your Parents: A Practical Guide to Eldercare,* by Nora Jean Levin, from the public library.

Here is a woman who is on top of things. From Nora I learn that long ago I should have been planning for what is happening to Daddy, I should have made lists of his assets, evaluated my resources, planned for legal and financial incapacity, and arranged for long-term care. I should have bought special insurance to cover that. I should have learned to "investigate using new technologies and adapting available devices to maintain your parents' independence or reduce functional impairments," as Nora instructs on page 8. I should have "plugged into networks" and "taken preventive measures."

Nora's book makes me feel like if I'd read it ten years ago, Daddy would be remembering things now. It is too late to do most of the things she suggests. What fascinates me is the part in her book on demographics. Daddy is not alone. There is an army of daddies gathering. They are about to attack the planet with incapacity. They will fill hospitals, they will suck the energy from families. They will envelop us in need.

Nora reported the same facts I read in *Newsweek* back in January. In 1900, the average American died at forty-seven; in 1987, he died at seventy-four; and today he lives eighty-three years. The number keeps climbing. Advances in medicine are keeping people alive longer. In 1900, there were 3 million Americans sixty-five or older; half a century later there were 33 million. Now those over eighty-five are the fastest-growing part of the population. As for Alzheimer's: 4 million people have it and the number is climbing exponentially. It is a crisis.

What that means to me is, I am not as alone as I feel. A huge mass of children—mostly daughters—will soon join me. Studies have shown that most of those millions of aging Americans will live at home, with their children caring for them. "Modern medicine has prolonged life—but it has not guaranteed health," writes Nora.

That is for sure.

People aren't prepared for what is coming. It will hit them as it has me. An army of the forgetful is about to march on the whole country, and nobody seems much concerned about it. They will forget their names, their addresses, their bank passwords. They will forget how to drive their cars, how to pilot their planes, how to turn on water, how to turn off their stoves. Some might have important jobs in nuclear power plants. Some might know scientific secrets, like how to make bombs. They will forget all this and then they will forget the names of their children and partners.

If it hasn't happened to you, then it must seem so abstract. The words *aging population* just don't have the urgent ring of *tornado, hurricane, famine,* or *flood.* But it is the same thing. Disaster is about to strike, hard and fast, and when it does it will leave us reeling and vulnerable as a society. It will cripple our medical system, it will absorb all sorts of resources. It will exhaust the whole nation.

Think of millions of people, each walking up or down their own Beartown Road with a person who raised them, trying to make it through each day, mourning the loss of once-bright minds. Some of them will be like me, simultaneously parenting their own children. Others will have just finished with that, sent their kids off to college, and just when they are feeling the dawn of independence, it will hit them. The end of life as they know it.

The memory project is what saves me.

I number Daddy's memories now and write them down in

a red notebook. They often repeat, and when they do I write them again. Sometimes in the repetitions they have details they didn't have the first time around.

Memory is so curious. Why can't I remember something one day and then recall it perfectly the next? What is this mental filing system? Why do some things, like colors and smells, seem so accessible, and other things—names, dates, events—so murky?

Why does one bright moment brim over from the past, out-shining others in the mental photo album of memory? Why do I so clearly possess a memory of the day I rode on the back of Michael Faris's motorcycle in the summer of 1973? If I shut my eyes I can feel the hot breeze ruffling my hair, the taste of Big Red gum in my mouth. It was neither significant nor notable. Yet there it is. I can see myself in a classroom at Columbia, at a lecture by Sandy McClatchy, my poetry professor. I can recall the exact inflection of his voice as he read us a poem by Yeats. It seems as though it just happened.

Some memories seem protected by their beauty. It is as though they have a coating of liveliness that no amount of time can touch. Like when I swam off St. John with my best friend, Julie, into a school of just-hatched baby sea turtles. Some of them brushed against us like soft hands on our arms and backs. Or the time I swam in a spring near a waterfall in Israel with Ilan Amir, an Israeli I had a brief, torrid affair with in the 1980s. I didn't much like him. He was handsome and arrogant and impatient. He took me swimming in the Mediterranean Sea in dangerous swells. I cut my knee on a rock and had to get nine stitches. He acted as though it were my fault.

Why do I remember Ilan, whom I did not love, and forget

so much about Richard Davidson, the California surfer turned architect, whom I did?

Why does Daddy so vividly remember his blistered hands and arms, wrapped in bandages seventy years ago, but forget me?

Having one's parents die is one of life's seminal experiences. It must bring on depression, despair, and a profound sense of loss. I know that someday, perhaps soon, I will face this. But having one's parent forget you, that is something altogether different. As a child and a teenager and even a young adult, so much of what we do is to please our parents. I recall the glint of pride in my father's eyes at my piano recitals, when I gave my Bas Mitzvah speech, when I delivered a lecture he attended in college. Those were important moments. Yet when I ask him now about each one, if he remembers them at all, he just says, "Nope, nope, nope."

I am lucky, I suppose, because I did not live to please my parents. I had a sense of self early on and understood that my parents would not always understand me. I think I even cherished the fact that they did not understand me. It meant I was an individual.

I knew as a child what I still know—that I could live without my parents. Without their awareness of me. And that is a good thing, because this is my life now. They either will or will not discover a cure for this disease before Daddy dies. My guess is probably not. I can live without Daddy recognizing me. I can do it.

In the *Newsweek* cover story, called "Alzheimer's: Unlocking the Mystery," they show pictures of brain scans. The warm colors are where the brains are "active." The dark purples, blues, and blacks are where they are not. The article is illustrated with three brains: a normal adult brain, one with late Alzheimer's, and a normal infant's brain. The normal adult brain hums with bright colors, a sunrise of activity. The brains of the late-Alzheimer's patient and the normal infant have dots of orange and yellow, but are mostly blue-black. The late-Alzheimer's brain "shows a dramatic lack of function," the diagram says. The late-Alzheimer's brain is being swallowed by beta-amyloid clusters of plaque, and the infant's brain is described as "not fully formed."

I can't help but notice that they are the same, almost identical, Ava and Daddy's brains. Maybe that is why I feel so alone here, left out of their club. They laugh and jabber; for an hour they throw a ball across a room. I try to play, too, but I feel outside the game. After a while Ava pushes me onto the couch. "Mommy sit," she says. She wants to play alone with Pop-pop. I am an intruder in their world of blue-black brains.

A mother watches her child learn and celebrates each orange flare of new ability. The first step, the first word, the first moment of conscious laughter. I don't mind that Ava and I are so different now, because I know she will be joining me little by little in the red-orange country of coherent thought. But with my father it is different. He is never coming back here. I feel so helpless against the beta-amyloid plaque clusters.

Jody tells me, "He is getting worse. He can't remember what to do with stairs."

Daddy has already forgotten forks and knives and cups and bowls. Now he is forgetting rooms and doors and ceilings and walls. He walks right into things as if they are not there. He has bruises.

On one of the first warm weekends of spring, Jody's husband, Dan, takes Daddy to a driving range. Daddy played golf competitively in college. He cannot hit the balls now. Later he tells me that he met this "golf guy." "He asked me to give him a few pointers, but my game isn't what it used to be."

My mother had explained away Daddy's increasing loss of memory as being due to the fact that "he just isn't interested in things." She insisted on this, year after year, that he was losing interest. She insists on this now. She says she cannot blame him, that the world is, in fact, boring. The two of them always had a snobbishness. Their city—Albuquerque—was droll and provincial, the people they knew mostly lacking.

This was a bad tactic, because it led to the day when he forgot her. Then she felt like he'd decided she was boring, too. That was insulting to her and made her angry.

I try to take a different view. I try not to take it personally that I no longer have a place in his brain. After reading about the plaque, about the way the bad molecules cleave to the good ones, exorcising memory in the process, I decide that I will try to look it more philosophically.

The best way to understand things sometimes is by their opposites. Darkness is dark because it is devoid of light. Silence is silence because of the absence of sound. My father is forgetful because of the absence of memories. Forgetting has become a part of who he is, so I decide to try to honor his forgetfulness. I try to love it. It defines his being these days, and sometimes I feel that to see him I have to look through it, a shuttered window. Underneath the forgetting lie a few remembered things, shoelaces, the way to hold a razor to shave, song lyrics he recalls, like "cockels and mussels"—but you have to catch them at the right moment of the day, when they shine through the slats.

Daddy is Daddy now because he forgets.

Ava, on the other hand, is Ava, more and more, because she remembers.

My daughter's brain is, for lack of a better word, hungry. It sucks up everything in its path, a sponge. She sees a round shape and says "balloon." She see a horse and says "nay nay." She remembers in which refrigerator drawer the grapes have been stored. She pops videotapes in the machine and rewinds, then hits Play. She remembers that she is not allowed to play with my perfume bottle on top of the dresser. I have counted and determined that she knows at least 237 words now, at seventeen months. That is not counting past and future tenses, of which she manages a few.

When my father retired from the University of New Mexico, he was very proud of the fact that he had never turned on a computer. Proud of his computer illiteracy. He was, perhaps, the last non-computer-using economist to walk the earth.

He does not know how to use a microwave oven, telephone, or answering machine. Trying to turn on the car radio, he flips on the heat. Trying to turn down the heat, he turns on the radio.

Meanwhile Ava is absorbing everything. I sometimes think every moment of her life is still there, in bright relief, within easy grasp. She knows where the radio is and how to turn on the heat in the car. She gets the telephone. The microwave. The television. She gets the locks on doors. She gets it. Life.

She even remembers nursing. She hasn't nursed since she

was nine months old, which is half of her lifetime away now. She still grabs for my breasts, tries to pull my shirt up and latch on. She laughs when she is doing it, like she knows she is being mischievous. "You are a big girl now, Ava," I say.

"No booby. Cup," she says.

She remembers Shane. She walks through the house pointing at the few remaining paintings of his on the walls. "Dadi, Dadi," she says. He used to take her with him into his studio and let her draw with big Conté crayons on his sketch pads. At Denny's, a waitress once gave her crayons and paper. She grabbed them and began scribbling furiously. "Painting Dadi," she said.

I wonder, will the neurons in her brain be affected, too? Will her brain become sticky with beta-amyloid clusters that interrupt the flow of past to present? Will she someday forget Daddy? Shane's paintings? Me?

It seems impossible that anything could be wrong with her, ever. But maybe somewhere on her DNA is a gene that will click on someday and start the process. The beginning of the end of her memory.

chapter 21

No Escape

>———∙<∘∘≻≺∘∘>∙———<

At approximately 3:45 on a Tuesday in late April it happens. John Steinbeck flies out of my head.

It is so disturbing I call a friend. "Who is that author," I ask, "who wrote about migrant laborers in the Depression . . . ? One book was really famous. . . . This family travels across the country to California—"

My friend interrupts, a note of horror in her voice. "*The Grapes of Wrath*? By Steinbeck?"

"Right," I say, in equal horror.

My brain has let go of *The Grapes of Wrath,* a classic of American literature. That is just great.

It is happening. I have Alzheimer's, too. The orange flares of healthy activity in my brain must be fading.

The fear is not irrational. It is based on fact. I hear it all the time, on television, on the radio; the paper I work for reported on it. Alzheimer's is, in some cases, genetically linked. In addition to his brown eyes, dark hair, and olive complexion, my father could have passed down to me his atrophied, shambled brain.

There is an advertisement on National Public Radio for an Internet search engine called Northern Lights. It is described as "a search engine that organizes, categorizes, prioritizes, and files information into blue custom-search folders." I think how beautiful it would be if I could just install Northern Lights into my father's brain. Into my brain. It would solve all our problems.

But even if such a thing could be done, my father would never let me. He has always loathed computers. It was unusual for him to feel that negative; he had always been very interested in all things—food, books, politics. Maybe he hated computers late in his career because he suspected that they could do what he was no longer able to do: retrieve.

This is dire information, because if Daddy had Alzheimer's, back then—when he was teaching—it means he had "early onset" Alzheimer's, and from the literature I have read, that is the worst kind. Worst for *me,* that is—because it is the kind that appears to be hereditary.

It would start with John Steinbeck, with *The Grapes of Wrath.* Then spread, like a stain.

All the time now I do this: I test myself. For everything I remember, I give myself points.

First-grade teacher: Not sure.
Second-grade teacher: Mrs. Bell
Third-grade teacher: Mrs. Clayton
Fourth-grade teacher: Mrs. Miller
Fifth-grade teacher: Mr. Powers
The original name of Istanbul: Constantinople

My mother's favorite candy: Barton's Almond Kisses
Tom Guralnick's cat: Cleo
Longest side of a triangle: hypotenuse
The parts of cells that power them: mitochondria.

I go over the names of all the streets I have ever lived on: Guadalupe Trail, Menaul, Lead, General Chenault. There is a street in Greenpoint, Brooklyn, that I can't remember. And one in Philadelphia, on a hill above the art museum, that I can't remember, either. They have gone into hiding in my mind, maybe gotten stuck behind something else. Still, when I add up my points, I do pretty well.

I cannot stop it, I am creating my own memory exam.

But what constitutes a reasonable slippage of memory, and what is a warning sign? Should I remember whole days intact from childhood?

Because I don't.

What were my favorite clothes? I remember certain patchy jeans. An amethyst angora sweater. A light-pink cotton dress. Where did the rest of the clothes of my life disappear to? I do not know.

Does this mean my mind is eroding? If I live my life with confidence, ignoring these gaps, does that make me as crazy as those people who continue to live in the houses on those cliffs in California until they drop off in a mud slide? Am I in denial, like my family was about Daddy?

I do not know.

For me, the strongest memories are associated with snow. How my mother came into the room I shared with my sister when I was a child and shook me gently: "Go and look out the window for a surprise," she'd say. We stood on our toes to peek out the high bedroom windows and saw the world, transformed overnight from Technicolor to black-and-white, like an old movie.

"If you get dressed now and have breakfast, you can go out and play before school," she'd say, and we would scramble to throw on sweaters and jeans and boots to run outside. We'd dish great armfuls of the dry, light, new snow into the sky and then fall down and make angels.

Worth ten points at least.

But does remembering that—in so much detail—mean I am safe? Could I be saved by a yard full of snow?

I hope so. But I do not know.

I am becoming a bit paranoid that I have it. I tell Samme, who is a health reporter, about this fear.

"Don't worry too much," she says. "For one thing, you are enormously stressed right now, which could cause memory lapses. Furthermore, they are very close to understanding Alzheimer's. Some doctors predict they will have a cure within seven years. If you actually do have it, and I doubt you do, they will likely have a cure in time to help you."

Seven years. That should be long enough. For me, at least.

But then I start thinking about what those seven years will be, those seven years I will wait for someone to save my brain. And despair kicks in. While I wait for my brain to be saved I will wipe spills, run errands, potty-train Ava, and watch my father, whose brain cannot be saved, fade slowly away.

It is too late for him. But what about me? What about my life? I will have no life.

I do, of course, have a life. I have a parent and a child, we eat macaroni and cheese for dinner, we go on walks, we watch *Sesame Street* together. Two of the three of us find it highly entertaining.

Meanwhile, spring is here, the air smells different, pungent and rich. Some days it is so powerful, I fight the urge to leave Ava with Jody, drop off Daddy at a hotel, and go out somewhere. I'd like to hit a bar. I daydream about the New Mexico State Fair cowboys, the sweet scent of horses and hay on their boots. Or the tattoed bikers at the bar on a certain corner of Brooklyn, smelling of motor oil and grease. Or a professor of lithography or a poet or a short-order cook. If only I could have one night away from this land of forgotten things, of missing pieces. Just to hang out in the free world, get tipsy, be weird and wear ridiculous faux snakeskin boots.

That part of my life, I am afraid, is over. I have had my last adventure, my last too-drunk walk downtown in the summer rain. My last conversation about ideas that makes me dizzy with its sentient leaps and wit.

There are some pluses about having one's life over. I will never again sit in a chair at a party and drink a glass of wine while someone bores me with an anecdote about the time they rode in an elevator with Brad Pitt. I will never again have a dinner conversation about the underappreciated ideas of Bakhtin. I will never have to listen to someone go on for too long about the loss to the world of Kurt Cobain. I will never have to listen to anyone apply Marxist theory to analyze game shows.

But also I will never again kiss someone on a subway platform in Manhattan. I am stuck here, on this farm I dreamed of, this lilac-clad house upon the hill in the densest part of nowhere. This paradise on its head. Because I am a caretaker.

It means people need me, all the time. The thought of it makes my skin prickle. It makes me sweat even when I am cold.

It appears that I am over.

I've been scheming to reclaim the smallest corner of myself. I steal time. I sneak away from work and go to movies in the middle of the day. I see sci-fi thrillers and stupid comedies. I see scary movies. They remove me from my life, if only for a few hours. Halfway through I get worried about things I should be doing and leave. But sometimes I stay. I put my feet on the seat in front of me in the empty theater and I eat popcorn and I watch the credits roll.

See, I tell myself. I have a life.

And I wake up before dawn, before Ava and Daddy, and go outside and run through the cemetery. I leave Samo inside, whining at the door. I want to be alone. I want to hear my feet thud and splash with no doggy echo. I want to be a person without baggage, if only for a few minutes. If only in a cemetery in the rain.

I run and run. Away from the man who has left me, and the baby he left behind. I run from the remains of the person who was my father. I run from his questions. I pound against the hard ground, I jump over briar patches, ripping socks. I climb a steep hill to a field full of tiny yellow flowers and tall purple stalks that poke through snowy patches. Loosestrife is blooming, it shouts with color.

Then I run to the edge of the forest and smell the trees. I look for bears.

. . .

Back at home I watch Ava sleep, feeling her dream. She is thirty-two inches long. Her thick, long eyelashes spread out across her cheeks like fans. There is not a freckle anywhere on her body. She is perfect. Watching her, I feel the need to escape, to run, to go, drain away from me.

I will be okay without a life for now. She is my life. For today, anyway, she is enough. Without a word or gesture, she takes away my desire to sneak to midday movies, to drink myself to oblivion on rum-and-Cokes in a suburban bar talking to calendar salesmen and men who drive trucks.

No, I will work and come home, to my baby and my father.

chapter 22

Learning to Wink

There is a story my father used to tell, about a student of his at the university. In one of his survey courses on labor economics, a discussion of Hegel and Kant turned existential. The meanings of currency, labor, and human toil were being debated—as usual—but the discussion expanded to include the very meaning of human life. It is what is supposed to happen in college: Students toss around great ideas and dive deep into pools of meaning. During this particular discussion, one student raised his hand and asked my father, "But Professor Cohen, how can I even know for sure that I exist?"

My father replied by asking the student, "Who is asking the question?"

I am reminded of this story when I walk into my father's bedroom and find him crying again, standing by the window, watching the April rain pour down.

"What's the matter, Daddy?" I ask.

"A fellow ought to know who he is," he says.

• • •

It has been eight months he has lived on Beartown Road with us. Still, each day he needs to be introduced to us afresh. Every morning when Ava tears into his room and wakes him, pulling his index finger to get him up, he blinks his eyes open and registers her presence. And I can see it, it is absolute, unadulterated surprise. He is surprised to see a baby. But he is delighted, too.

She, on the other hand, has no confusion about his identity ("Pop-pop!"). There is a look on her face when she sees him. She recognizes. She is sure about him.

As long as she is right in front of him, he can keep track of the fact of her. But if she leaves the room for a minute, he needs to know all over again "where the little guy came from." And whose baby it is.

Jody thinks sometimes Daddy is afraid that Ava may be his child. In some ways she is. He is the dominant male in her life. They often cuddle on the couch and look at books. Although he turns the pages and tells the story, I have noticed lately that the story he tells has nothing to do with the actual book they are reading.

This has led me to the suspicion that he is losing a cherished skill: the ability to read.

I remember once seeing a woman on the subway doing a crossword puzzle with extreme concentration. She scribbled and erased and scribbled again, blackening the boxes with letters until almost all were filled in. Standing behind her I was able to see that the puzzle she was doing was upside down, and her answers, from my vantage point, appeared to have no relevance to the puzzle. In fact they weren't even words. The whole thing was a one-act play she was performing for the other passengers on the train. She was illiterate, pretending.

When Daddy reads to Ava he turns pages, scans sentences; all the booklike movements are in place, glasses balanced on his nose just so, but the words are all wrong. Not even close.

It is a performance.

Spring is here. First came the crocuses, daffodils, and wild irises; and those tiny flowers that hug the ground in the cemetery have begun to show their heads. Now comes the main event. Interestingly, Daddy recognizes spring before me. "Buds," he says, pointing to the lilac bushes that flank the house. And to Ava's delight we go outside without jackets. Daddy and Ava jump in puddles. Jody has bought her yellow pull-up galoshes. "Boom," Ava says, each time she jumps.

I stand aside, smiling and watching them, thinking about all the laundry I will have to do. This morning when I woke up, Daddy was in bed with us, curled up under the covers in a fetal position. Ava was cuddled inside his arms.

It occurs to me that what we are is a family. We are cozy, the seasons wrap their weather around us.

Somewhere near here the bears must be stirring in their dens, stretching their bear arms, yawning great bear yawns. They are beginning to awake from the long slumber of winter. Perhaps they will venture out to see what is going on in the world. Maybe they will see us and know we made it through. Maybe they will be happy to know that the humans on top of the hill survived snow and ice and cold and fear.

• • •

In a corner of Shane's studio I have discovered an imaginary world. Now that it is warmer, I venture inside there more often, usually at night, after Daddy and Ava are asleep.

The world is made of tiny toys, mud, and bricks. Thumb-size soldiers are waging war on a castle. There are people traveling on a road, carrying baskets of hay on their backs. There are men engaging in some kind of tournament, and a man in shackles being tried before a prince. There are people standing around a fire in the smallest forest, made of sticks. They are toys made by a company called Playmobil. The people have so much detail, tiny hats with plumes, suits of armor, and flags etched with coats of arms.

He must have spent hours arranging them. I knew that in between paintings he'd spent time doing this, but I never stopped to really examine it the way I do now. There are wizard people and witches standing around a cauldron. There are guerilla warriors perched on plateaus made of apple juice cartons. He has carts and horses and kings and princesses.

He made a world outside the world of us. It is quite elaborate. Long ago, he must have felt a need to escape.

I wonder if Shane will remember us in a distant future.

Will the smell of baby wipes and stale apple juice bring back Ava? Will anything at all remind him of me? I wonder if he thinks of us now.

Lately I have been doing really sick things, like rereading his e-mails to Marty and calling all his friends. I talk to Jeremiah and Jonathan for hours. They tell me Marty and he are already over. They say it was just a fling, a couple of weeks, and that he is beside himself with grief at his mistake. That he carries Ava's picture with him everywhere and talks endlessly about us, about the house on Beartown Road, his studio. They say he sleeps all day and draws in his notebooks. That is his life. He tried to get a job at Denny's but it somehow fell through. He got a job working for the Census Bureau but was fired after the Jeep broke down. He is broke and depends on his friends for meals. They say he has slept on other people's couches for months. This is what they tell me, but I have not decided yet if I believe it.

He called one night, for the first time in months. I had been waiting so long to hear from him it was anticlimactic. I had forgotten all the things I wanted to say. I put Ava on with him. She said, "Hi, Da," and then got distracted by a toy. Good for her. I could hear him crying on the other end.

Shane has just thrown away a winter of memories. When he is old he will probably not want to remember this time, how he walked away from his baby girl. He has created the sort of memories people do not want to have.

Or maybe not. Maybe his friends are wrong, maybe he and Marty are so blissful that he has a whole collection of beautiful new memories.

In spite of myself I want to tell him things, like how Ava can climb in her high chair herself and how she is so affectionate. "Kiss Mommy," she says, and throws her arms around me. I want to tell him how she asks me for Jell-O and cereal and bananas. I want to tell him that she can wink. Daddy loves it and winks back at her. They have marathon wink sessions that leave me in stitches.

But whenever I have called one of Shane's friend's houses where I think he might be staying and he answers, I just hang up. What do you say to someone who walked out on you and your kid seven months earlier? "How's it going? By the way, your daughter can wink."

One time when we did talk, he asked me why I didn't call him on his birthday.

"I forgot," I said.

It was the first time I ever got any real pleasure out of the thought of forgetting something.

chapter 23

The Bolivian Incident

>———⋅⟨◇◇⟩⋅———<

It is seventy degrees out, the end of April. Perhaps by habit we are still afraid to go out without coats. So we go on our walks wearing them anyway, sweating.

I picked up Twyla this morning in the front yard and noticed she was heavier than usual, her round belly swollen and the nipples stiff and enlarged.

"Oh for Pete's sake," I said aloud.

"What?" Daddy asked.

"The cat is pregnant."

"Just what we need—more cats," he said. When I tell Jody I want her to look into a kitty abortion, her anti-abortion sentiments surface with fury. "I'll give away the kittens when they come," she declares, practically through tears.

"Okay," I say. "If you promise to do that, then we keep the pregnancy. But I mean *promise*. I can't handle another responsibility."

• • •

Daddy asks me every day now when the kittens are coming, if they were born in the night. I put Ava's hand on Twyla's belly and say Twy-twy is going to be a Mommy. She totally gets it. "Baby kitties!" she says. "Yay!" She claps her hands.

She has discovered that the cats amuse her. She remembers all the places they like to curl and sleep. I see her looking for them under couches and behind curtains. She calls for them. "Ticky, ticky, ticky," she says.

I have begun to think of her baby brain as a gluey flytrap. Nothing escapes. It is a giant sponge. I drop an iron on my foot. "Shit," I swear. For the next week she drops things, watching my reaction. "Sit, sit, sit," she says. It is an exercise that causes her to convulse in laughter. She knows it makes me wince. She loves that.

Ava has discovered power. She knows already that words are dangerous. She has realized she can own them and use them over and over to elicit certain reactions in me. So she does.

She has also discovered climbing. She was the sort of baby who could never be happily contained in a crib. She vetoed the idea from birth. She has an inherent need for freedom, abandon, thrill. She likes to spin around and around until she gets so dizzy she falls. She likes to hang off the bed backward, her head upside down, laughing and laughing. She likes to pile things up and climb them. She pushes the chair over from the table and clambers up it, then makes her way onto the counter. I have walked in on her several times midclimb. She wants to see how high up she can get and what it feels like up there. It is my job to drag her down to earth. To ruin the fun. "No, no, no!" she screams when I disassemble her climbing apparatus.

• • •

Daddy really cares about the memory project now. The way Ava wants to climb, he wants to remember. As the bright green buds expand into leaves, and tulips dust the yard, he has a mission—he wants to prove to me that he can recall things. He volunteers memories all the time. Most are sharp, focused, detailed. They are also over sixty years old.

"How about this," he says proudly. "Mrs. McCosland."

"What about her?" I ask.

"She was my first-grade teacher, how about that!"

"Wow."

"First grade. Can you remember the name of *your* first-grade teacher?"

"No, can you?"

"Can I what?"

"Can you remember the name of *my* first-grade teacher?"

My father looks puzzled.

"You were there," I say. "You must have met her."

"Really? Well, I don't remember that. Why would I be there?"

"Because you are my father," I say.

As usual: "I am?"

Daddy remembers Mrs. McCosland, he remembers the look of his street in Cleveland, the layout of the house, the way his "bubbie" smelled—of schmaltz and lilac perfume—his mother's hands, the fine white dust that rose off his father when he came home from a day of plastering. He tells me he can remember food: his mother's challah, her apple strudel, her brisket, a good pastrami sandwich he ate in Cleveland.

He can recall his neighborhood friends. For our memory project, he tells me how once they tricked him into siphoning gas from a car and he accidently swallowed some. He can vividly recall the experience of burping gasoline-smelling burps for weeks, he says.

But he cannot remember me.

He cannot remember my sister, Melanie, or my half-brother, Jon, his son from his first marriage. Sometimes, he cannot even remember my mother, Julia. He is getting worse.

"Did I ever tell you about the time I was kidnapped in Bolivia?" he asks me one evening.

"Tell me again, Daddy."

"Well, it was the 1960s, around the time of Kennedy and all that craziness. I was working on a rather important State Department project, down in Bolivia. We were trying to help them straighten out their economy, help them with their currency and labor relations. Oh, it was a mess, all tangled up. And Julia, she went on a little vacation with a friend, a sight-seeing thing, up to Lake Titicaca. All of the sudden these people—they were farmers, agricultural workers, all mad because their prices were bottoming out, they wanted certain government concessions— they burst in and took us hostage! It was a couple of days—me and a couple other guys, all Americans, in this dull room. The men were outside most of the time, and we were in there with these peasant women. They were really quite mean to us, ordering us about and all, and giving us just this dull gruel. Yelling at us. We had to sleep on hard desks. You know," he said contemplatively, "we weren't sure what was going to happen. Then all of the sudden this guy—a Jewish guy from New York City— came down. All on his own. He came and negotiated with these folks and they let us go!"

Daddy is remembering. He shuts his eyes. "There were

216 · Elizabeth Cohen

news guys there from all over, cameras, interviewing us. It was an international incident. This guy got us out, he got these farmers and growers some concessions of some sort and then he got on a plane and took off. I never heard about him again.

"Julia arrived right there at the end, she didn't even know what was going on. She was stunned. We walked out on some kind of tarmac. They took our pictures. We were sort of heroes."

"Wow," I say.

"Yeah, it was something."

"Where was I during all this?"

"You? You weren't there. I didn't even know you then."

I decide to fight back, just this once. Because I know I must have been there. I was five. I was in kindergarten. Melanie and I had a Bolivian nanny named Clara. "You did know me, I was there," I said.

"No, I didn't," he says, sure of himself.

"I had a nanny . . . named Clara."

"You must be talking about someone else. My daughters. They were there, not you."

"I am your daughter."

"My daughters," he says, "are little tiny girls."

My mother calls. "Was Daddy kidnapped in Bolivia?" I ask her.

She laughs. "No, but his best friend was. It was quite an incident. We were really scared. Some workers wanted attention for their strike and kidnapped a few Americans. Daddy's friend was one of them."

My mother has gone back to Albuquerque from Seattle to try to sell the house and go over their taxes with an accountant. But once there, she immediately became sicker; the real estate agent has to get her food and drive her to the doctor. She can't even get around.

On the phone she tells me, "I have made a decision, I am coming to Daddy," she says.

"What do you mean?"

"I mean I have a ticket. I am coming there."

"You are?"

I feel a bit shocked by this news. It isn't as if I'm not happy, I just feel rattled. Daddy, Ava, and I are sort of a team now. We have gotten things in some sort of order. In the morning I make him coffee and toast while Ava eats Cheerios in her high chair. I give him his pills and Ava her vitamin drops. We sing "Old McDonald Had a Farm" together. I feel ready to face the day.

I try to imagine my mother in our house, with the baby, Daddy, dog, cats, and boxes. How would she get up and down the steep staircase? She'd hate my bathrooms. She'd hate the woods.

I won't tell her about the bears.

My mother's real estate agent calls me and says that my mother is very sick. She wants to take her to the hospital but my mother won't go. Instead she wants to come here and find a doctor. "I bought my ticket already and I am coming," my mother says definitively. "I'll be there on the sixth. It is probably just a couple of cracked ribs." She has had cracked ribs before. "There is nothing they can do about them. I miss Daddy," she says.

She talks to my father for hours. I listen to their conversations. "I miss you," Mommy says. "I love you."

"Well, it's about time," he says. "Come right over. We'll take care of you."

She says she'll be coming after she wraps up a few things.

The real estate lady thinks she should come sooner, or she might not make it at all.

When they get off the phone, Daddy asks me if I have a picture of my mother. But his eyesight is bad; he can't see the pictures I've hung on his walls, and the snapshot I find to hand him is old, from 1977. "That is my wife! She is really attractive," Daddy says admiringly.

Then he turns to me, his eyes tearing up. "Please help me out here, what is her name? Can you believe I can't remember a thing like that!"

"Julia," I say. "Her name is Julia Cohen."

Ava, who parrots everything these days, walks into the kitchen where Daddy has hung up the phone. "Juco," she says.

"Tell me," Daddy says, "has she ever seen this little one here? I think she'd get a real kick out of him."

chapter 24

A Black Thing, and Stars

————— ⋖◆H◆⋗ —————

My father has decided he likes the adult day care program. "I am teaching again," he says. "A group of older folks, a little dull but very nice. I sang for them."

Although rainy all the time, it is getting much warmer now and we have finally exchanged our big coats and jackets for slickers and windbreakers. Daddy asks me in the morning what to wear, what he is supposed to be lecturing about. I tell him it is just open discussion, no focused topic. "Good," he says. "Because I have lost my notes."

He asks me to help him don professorial gear. A suit and tie. He has adopted one of Ava's diaper bags as his "briefcase." I find it, filled with old papers and paid bills that I left on my desk. "I wonder if anyone will show up? The weather is awful," he says.

He is right, the rain is torrential. The meteorologists are calling for flooding of local rivers. "April showers bring May flowers," Daddy says. And then, "You look nice."

220 • *Elizabeth Cohen*

Jody arrives to drive him to class, as she does three days a week now. She usually takes him for a bagel first. He likes it with lox and cream cheese. They go to a place called Best Bagel in Town. He thinks that is funny. "Best Bagel! We'll have to see about that," he says. "We'll do some bagel research."

At the adult day program, Daddy keeps making things for Mommy. He remembers that she is coming and asks me about it every day: "When is my mother expected?"

In adult day care, Daddy glues cotton balls onto cardboard rabbits, weaves ribbons through the holes in a plastic basket, reminding me of my "sewing cards" when I was a child. "How do you think she'll like that?" he asks.

I tell him she'll love it. He wins her a jar of bath beads and some soap in bingo. Apparently he is quite the life of the party. The other day when Jody picked him up, he asked her to wait a minute. He ran back inside the building and sang one more refrain of a song they had been singing.

"Okay, now we can go," he said when he came back out again.

Although his memory has not improved, his mood has. It is probably the Prozac, but I like to think it's us, our life, Ava and me and Samo. Or maybe just knowing, somewhere deep inside the blue-black mass of his brain, that my mother is coming.

You never stop hoping. You never know for sure.

⸻

"Hey," Daddy says. "Can I ask you something personal?"

I hate when he says things like that.

"You aren't a bad-looking woman. What about guys? You have a special guy hanging around? I never see any."

"No, no special guys. I am still married."

"You know what I think about that?" he asks. "I think that is a lost cause, this so-called husband. He calls you?"

"No," I say.

"He sends you a little check, for that baby?"

"No."

"He is a good-for-nothing. No disrespect. But a guy like that, well, I'd advise you not to be thinking of that one. Chances are he won't change."

"Okay, Daddy," I say. "I'll keep that in mind."

"Better off without him."

His words are so certain. They are sharp and sure and sting me in a place I try not to feel.

When we go on walks now, we bring umbrellas. Daddy fiddles with them, can't figure out how to open them up. "Damn complex machinery."

When we go out, Samo bounds into puddles and then comes back and jumps on us, covering us in his muddy footprints. On a Saturday when the rain stops for a whole afternoon, the dog bounds away and barks, like he can see something beyond the graveyard where we are walking. He flies through the brush and digs furiously at a fence until he explodes onto the other side and then barks. "Probably sees something," Daddy conjectures. "Probably a squirrel."

I peer through the woods after Samo. There is a cracking noise below us in the trees and the sound of Samo barking again. Then the cracking stops and Samo rushes back to us. He has a look on his dog face like he wants to tell us something. I think that perhaps he's seen them—the bears.

Maybe they live down there in the woods, beyond the Wrights' pond. Maybe they were out splashing in the puddles, too. It is universal, spring. Something all creatures appreciate. Barn swallows are making a nest on the front porch. The baby and Daddy want to be outside all the time.

"Side!" Ava demands. "Side!"

And Daddy says, "Did you hear that? He is learning words, he is really coming along!"

I walk to the edge of the trees and look through shadows and brush. I imagine I can see, down below us, a dark thing that moves. The moving darkness cracks twigs. It makes a shuffling sound.

I round up my family to head back to the house. Although I think of the bears as my friends, it has suddenly dawned on me that bears might actually be dangerous.

As we cross the road we see the Wrights in their front yard with all their grandchildren. Everyone has come out to enjoy the day. They wave us over. The little girls adore Ava and play chase with her while Daddy and I talk to their grandfather. Mr. Wright is very nice to my father. A few times when I have left Daddy in the rocking chair on the front porch to smoke, I have looked out the window and seen him down by the road, engaged in a conversation with Mr. Wright. Although I do not know for sure, I imagine they talk mostly about weather. Maybe Mr. Wright is telling my father the story of his old barn that was burned down years ago.

Mr. Wright waves me over and tells me to go in the kitchen and say hello to Danielle. I take Ava with me and together we knock on the front door. "Knock, knock, knock," Ava says. Soon Betty Wright answers. "Come on in, Elizabeth," she says. "We're making cookies."

Danielle stands by the stove next to baby Marky. Over the winter, while his sister has learned how to use a prosthesis, he has learned to walk. Ava goes over to him and takes a toy out of his hand. He starts to cry. "Ava, please give Marky back his toy," I say. "That isn't nice."

Ava looks at me and says, "No. Mine."

Then Danielle walks over and expertly exchanges Marky's toy for a cookie. You can tell she is the eldest of five children. She knows the cardinal rule of children: distraction, distraction, distraction.

Danielle's long wheat-colored hair falls across her shoulder when she leans over. I try hard not to look at the place where her arm should be.

"Danielle is doing so good," Betty says, sensing my unease. "All our girls are."

Danielle looks up at me and smiles meekly. Although she is only ten years old, she has great dignity and grace. She makes me see outside the circle of our circumstances.

When we leave, Mr. Wright takes me aside and tells me some news. "We are going to be heading out of here. We put the place on the market. We've got some interest."

"I don't know how we'll live without you here," I say. I mean it.

"Well, the place is just too big for us now. The Parkinson's is going to get worse, and my son's family—with Danielle and all—well, they need us. We'll put up a double-wide over there."

"Well at least you won't be too far away. I'll be dropping by," I say.

"Please," he says to me, and pats me on the back. "Please do."

Later, after Daddy and Ava have fallen asleep, I walk outside. I sit on the porch and look at the Wrights' house, where the only light in a center room blinks off. Then I walk to the edge of the forest with Samo and look through the trees for the moving darkness. But you cannot see dark inside dark. It is completely quiet.

The rain has left a damp, musty smell that combines with something pungent and sweet. The lilacs are coming out. I have never felt so happy about lilacs. Their tight buds unfolding excite me. In a few days we will live in a perfumed world.

The lilacs are the purple ribbons tied at the gate of spring. The hardest winter of my life is over. In the distance is the untuned banjo twang of a few frogs in the Wrights' pond. And beyond them, the night, crammed with stars.

Stars and lilacs connect us to people. We are not as alone as we feel. The same stars blink over the Wrights' house, over the people who have lost their homes in the floods in Mozambique. Somewhere across the country those stars are shining over the heads of my mother and Shane. Her lilac bushes must be blooming, too. We couldn't be farther from one another, but despite all that has happened, we are still connected, by stars, by night, by spring.

When I come back in, I hear the cats crying. Lulu and Milo are standing around the food bowls in the kitchen with that expectant look. But Twyla is missing.

"Twy-twy," I call out. I click the spoon on the side of the cat food can. That usually brings her streaking in. She has been constantly hungry since she got pregnant, eating two to three meals a day. But no Twyla comes running. "Twy-twy," I yell again.

I start hunting around the house. I look in all the usual places: Behind the sofa on the windowsill, in my bed, atop the woodstove. Finally I open my closet. There is Twyla, curled on a sheet with four of the tiniest creatures I have ever seen tucked beside her. They are smaller than my thumb, with pink legs wagging off their tummies like confetti. She turns on her side. At that very moment she is birthing another kitten. In the dim light shining from the hallway I watch as it slips onto the sheet, sheathed in afterbirth. Two grays, two splotchies, and now this one, tiny and white, vibrating with cold. I run downstairs and turn up the heat.

I almost smack into Daddy as I fly down the stairs. He is standing in the living room, stark naked. "I had a sort of terrible accident," he says.

I toss a robe at him from the laundry room. "What happened?"

"I lost control."

"Daddy, Twy-twy is having her kittens—now!"

"Oh my!" he says, following me up the stairs. We tiptoe into the bedroom and crouch beside the closet door, which I crack open. We peer in. Just as we do, a sixth kitten, another white one, is being born. "Wow," I whisper.

"Would you look at that," he says.

But this kitten, unlike the others, doesn't move or wiggle, tremble or start rutting for a nipple. It just lies there.

"Something is wrong with it," I say.

Without pause, Daddy reaches into the closet, picks up the tiny white creature, and puts it in the palm of his hand. With his forefinger he rubs its back and then turns it over and rubs its tummy. "Nothing," he says.

Together, we walk downstairs. I open a shoe box and Daddy places the dead kitten inside. I tell him I will bury it in the yard in the morning.

"Five is enough," my father says. Then he remembers something: "I don't mean to be a bother, but I need a bit of help."

When we go upstairs I look in his room. He *has* had an accident. There is shit all over his bed. "I made a bad mess," he said. "Can we clean it up somehow?"

I put him in a hot shower, strip the sheets, and make the bed afresh. He's done this on two former occasions and once in Jody's car. I wonder if he is sick, or if what I read in an article on the progress of Alzheimer's is happening—I wonder if he is losing control of his bowels.

In the morning while I wash the dirty sheets, Ava looks for Twy-twy. She is her favorite cat. I discuss it with Daddy and Jody and we decide not to tell her about the kittens yet. She is too young, she will want to hold them. Fragility is something she does not understand. "When they get bigger we'll tell him," Daddy says, sort of proud to be in on this decision.

At his adult day program they have told him he is not paid, he is not the teacher. They explained to Jody that they will not lie to him. He is devastated, angry. "Why did you tell me that?" he demands. "There is a fellow there who told me that we pay *them!*"

"He is wrong, Daddy," I say. "He is just an underling. You get paid by the people at the top. That man doesn't even know about it."

I will lie all day to protect my father's ego, to protect him from pain. I would tell him we lived on the moon.

He accepts my explanation, but he has decided the place is "cockamamy." He will not go there again.

chapter 25

The Forgettery

>———————⊰◆◆◆⊱————————<

Daddy and I drive to Syracuse to pick up my mother. I leave Ava with Jody, thinking that way I can better help with the suitcases. I have no idea how much stuff she is bringing.

We drive in a downpour through pockets of deep fog. We can't see the cars in front of us, and when big trucks go by they send obscuring waves of water onto the windshield. We go about forty-five miles per hour the whole way, and Daddy keeps saying, "I hope we won't miss my mother," as though Mommy will be there only for a moment and if we don't arrive precisely at that moment she will disappear.

We have only one conversation the whole two-hour drive, but we repeat it several times, taking turns with the question and answer. The conversation goes like this:

Me, and then later, Daddy: *"Do you think Mommy will like it here?"*
Daddy first, and then me: *"Probably not."*

My mother has a cantankerous soul.

The thunderstorm has the effect of putting him into a certain alert mode I have seen on a few occasions. He remembers better when things aren't going right. Like now. The hard rain, the cracks of thunder and lightning bolts make him remember Mommy and our current mission to pick her up. He won't even let me stop in Cortland for coffee. "Let's just get there," he says.

We arrive just in time, her plane is landing as we pull up. We park and rush through the airport to her gate, where people are deboarding.

Lots of families come off the plane, mothers with children, babies, and flight attendants. Then nobody. No Mommy.

"Oh God," Daddy says. "She is lost."

But then she appears, my mother, walking very slowly. She looks smaller than I ever remember, weak and unsteady. The widow's hump created by her disintegrating spine and osteoporosis seems more pronounced than ever.

"There she is!" he exclaims. "She made it!"

My mother, pulling a wheeled suitcase and carrying a big cloth bag, collapses into Daddy's arms. "Oh honey, they made me change planes in Chicago."

"Well, you are here now," Daddy says.

My mother stays in my father's arms and they stand there for what seems like a very long time.

As we get in the car I see that my mother is very sick. "How far is it? How long is the drive?" she asks. Her hands are trembling. She says she feels like she might throw up. "I am so glad to see Daddy," she says. "It was a terrible trip but it was worth it."

I make a decision. I pull up at the airport hotel. I will check us in and then I can evaluate how badly she is doing. "We're staying right here tonight, Mommy. You've had enough traveling for one day."

"Oh please," she says. "Don't make me angry."

"Don't get angry, just go along."

I pull her suitcases out of the car and check us in. In the room she collapses. Daddy looks helpless. "I feel so dizzy," she says.

"Do you feel like maybe you need to see a doctor or go to a hospital?" I ask. "Or can you rest up here and feel better?"

"I have felt this way for days," she says. "Nothing seems to help."

Daddy takes off Mommy's shoes and puts her feet up on the bed. He gets her a glass of water. "Just sit here by me, let me see you," she says to him, holding on to his arm. "Let me touch you."

My mother puts her hands on my father's face and he holds her close to him.

I call Jody from the room. "We're staying over. My mom is weak," I say.

"Did he remember her?" Jody asks. She has become fond of my father. She worried how this reunion would go.

"Turns out love is stronger than Alzheimer's, he totally knows who she is," I say.

My father is waving me into the bathroom, he wants to tell me something. "Hold on, Jody," I say, putting the phone on the bed.

"What, Daddy?" I walk into the bathroom.

He whispers, "This woman on the bed in there. I think she is very sick. Maybe we should get her some help."

I feel my chest tighten, a tingle in my neck. I pick up the phone again.

"Strike that," I say. "This is going to be a long night. Can you give Ava a kiss and tell her I will see her in the morning?"

"Sure," Jody says. And wishes me luck.

———⋙◈⋘———

My mother has brought a canvas bag of pills with her from New Mexico. She has mixed them all together in different bottles and baggies. They have words written on them, like *sleep, pain, constipation,* and *bones.* When I look at their dates they go back as far as the 1980s. "Mom, what are all these?" I ask her.

"Don't talk to me like that," she says. "Don't sound so exasperated."

When we get home I soon discover she takes pills all the time. She is especially fond of Tylenol 3 with codeine, and she is almost out. "I need you to get me some more of these," she says.

I call my sister. "What is up with all these pills?"

"She needs them," my sister says. "Don't try to take them away."

"I won't, but what are they all for?"

"Pain. She has pain, okay? She's old."

"I know that. But what about these Tylenol 3's?"

"They're for pain, okay?"

"I think she may be addicted to them."

"Well duh, that would be stating the obvious," says my sister.

I call Dr. Eder. "We need an immediate appointment," I say. His assistant makes one for us in the afternoon. I put Daddy,

Ava, and Mommy in the car and we drive to Chenango Bridge, to Eder's office. On the way it begins to snow. "What is this?" my mother asks. It is May, she points out.

"I know, Mom, I don't know why it is snowing. I am sorry it's snowing."

It is a freak storm. A spring storm, in May. The snow quickens, sheets of ice coat the wet roads. "Oh God, where the hell are we, Alaska?" Mommy asks.

I think of the lilacs, the fragile daffodils in the front yard, the cats, the bears. "I hope that the flowers are all right."

"I hope I am all right," my mother says.

We file into Dr. Eder's office. He walks in and looks at us. We are a motley crew. Ava is wearing her pajamas. Daddy is wearing the same clothes he has had on for days. I see my own reflection. I look frightful. I push down my hair, which is sticking out on one side in a weird, tangly puff. "So what have we here?" he asks.

I introduce him to my mother. "She has come to live with us for a while," I say.

"I am here for good," she says. "To be with my husband." She takes my father's hand. Daddy looks pleased.

Dr. Eder asks Mommy what exactly is bothering her. "Could you help us sort through her medications?" I ask. I have put all her pills into Ava's old Easter basket. There are about forty bottles in all. One by one we go through them. "It isn't a good idea to mix these together, Mrs. Cohen," he says. Some of the bottles contain several different pills. "We can't tell what they were prescribed for this way."

"I know what they're for," she says. "These little blue ones were for when I got my tooth pulled, and I am hanging on to them," she says. "The yellows are good for something to do with my heart." My mother tells him she wants more Tylenol 3's.

"Is that a good idea?" I ask.

"Shut up," my mother whispers at me. Then, to Dr. Eder, "I need them for pain."

We go over all her medical conditions, her bones, her back, her heart, her lungs. Dr. Eder says he'll send her to specialists to evaluate each problem. In the meantime, he writes out prescriptions for Tylenol 3 and Lorazapam. He gives her Serzone for depression. "These will help stabilize her, and then we'll see if we can get her on better pain medications that address her pain more specifically."

He throws out the basket of pills. My mother nearly leaps from her seat. "I need those," she says.

"They are old, Mrs. Cohen. They don't work very well after a while. We'll get you the right ones."

Mommy is having trouble with the stairs. She can't stand the cats. The little kittens are bigger now, they venture out of the closet sometimes and have a tendency to get underfoot. This delights Ava, who runs after them and sends them scurrying, clawing their way up curtains and beds.

From the moment she first saw the kittens, Ava has loved them, but with their sharp little claws that seem permanently bared, they present a problem. They hurt. Still, she can't resist them and has the long thin scabs to show for it.

"Why baby kitty hurt Ava?" she wants to know.

"I can't live like this," my mother says.

I call my sister. "What should I do?"

"Try to find a good place they can live nearby."

"They?"

"Well, you didn't think she was coming all that way to be apart from him, did you?"

The thought of Daddy leaving our house throws me off-guard. It surprises me how much it devastates me. "He likes it here," I say. "I have labeled all the rooms. We have a system here that is working."

"Well, label the rooms somewhere else," Melanie says. "He can't tell where he is anyway."

Mommy complains nonstop. She has determined that this is a terrible place. The only consoling thing is that she hated Albuquerque and Seattle, too. She hates everywhere.

Among the things she hates here is the fact that the spring snow is covering the ground. "First I live with one daughter under a wet rock and now I live with the other in a Christmas card," she says.

She tells me we have to find them an apartment or something immediately. "I can't stand it here, this is an awful house. I can't believe you bought it," she says.

She has shared with me her theory of Daddy. It is interesting. She has turned the deficits in his memory into assets. "He has a good forgettery," she says.

"What is a forgettery?"

"The opposite of a memory," she explains, as if talking to an idiot. "I have a good one, too."

The forgettery is the place where memories go once they disappear from the conscious mind, she says. Sort of a nest, somewhere in the brain. My mother tells me she has been observing and that I have a good forgettery, too. "You forget to call, you forget things I need, you forget all the time."

I don't want to think I have Alzheimer's. I don't want my mother to think I have Alzheimer's, either. I tell her I remember a lot of things, and then I bore her with details: people's names, our addresses and phone numbers from childhood. I tell her all our zip codes and describe the kitchen counters in each of our three houses as well as an apartment where we lived when Daddy was on sabbatical in Venezuela. I describe the porch of our house in Puerto Rico—another sabbatical—and the backyard of our neighbors the Jillsons, on General Chenault, as well as the tree that Craig Jillson fell out of and broke his arm.

I sing for my mother—"Daydream Believer" by the Monkees. It was my very first 45, which I played over and over on the tiny plastic record player I got for my birthday in the fifth grade.

I recite Hebrew, from my Bas Mitzvah. I sing her "HaTikvah." I sing the lyrics from the Weavers' album she and my father used to play when I was a child.

"That is very interesting," she says, "but what about French? Do you remember any of the French from those French lessons I paid for?"

I have to admit, I do not.

I try not to care about her words. We used to have screaming fights when I was younger, but now we don't. I swallow the poisonous things she says. They stick in my throat, but I do not react. She is quite sick. She requires empathy. She missed my father. And he seems so calm and comfortable around her. He hasn't had any more accidents.

Plus, she plans his outfits better than I do and helps him find things. She micromanages, handing him strips of dental floss and his toothbrush. She pats down his hair with water and trims his ear hairs. The entire time he lived with me alone, I never trimmed his ear hairs.

It irritates me in a way, how she has taken over his life, but I can see that for him it is a relief. He complies with her instructions like a man who has lost his sight and depends on a Seeing Eye dog. She fills the gap between remembering and forgetting with instructions and small tasks, which he often fails at. Nevertheless she keeps at him. It is "brain exercise," she says.

He is so quiet and docile now. Sometimes before he speaks he looks over at her, as if to ask permission. You can tell he is terribly afraid he'll offend her.

And when he gets things wrong, brings her a hairbrush when she asks for a glass of water or puts his shoes on the wrong feet, she explodes: "Stupid! That is just stupid!"

And although I cringe when she yells at him, I have to see it from his point of view. He wants the help. I felt a need to protect my father's dignity: I felt that my leaving him alone, uncorrected, would be a sign of respect. But left to his own devices he only felt scared and confused. My mother doesn't make room for confusion. She preempts it.

So I swallow the poison. I tell her I will help her. She loves my father and he loves her.

⸺⸺⸺

During lunch hours, after work, and before work, I take Mommy and Daddy to retirement homes and assisted living facilities. Places with names like Hilltop and Elizabeth Church Manor and the Ideal Senior Living Center. Each time, she tells the administrators, "Just tell me you have an empty room. I don't need to look around. When can I move in?"

But there are waiting lists. There are forms to be filled out. None of them have immediate openings. She gets angry. "Why do I want to see places that don't have openings?" she asks.

When we get to Castle Gardens, an assisted-living facility in nearby Vestal, they say they have an empty apartment. My mother says, "Great, we're moving in."

"Don't you want to see it?" I ask.

"No, we're moving in," she says. She tells Janet, the administrator, that she wants to move in right then. "Well, we need to clean it, Mrs. Cohen, but you can move in at the end of the week," Janet says.

"Great. That's what I want to hear," Mommy says.

We sit in the library of Castle Gardens and fill out forms. Daddy asks where we are and what we are doing. "Are these people lawyers?" he whispers to me.

"No, Daddy, it is just an apartment complex. You are moving in here."

"Oh, I see. Well, that's good. She'll like that!" he says, glancing over at my mother.

I tell my mother I think she is rushing. "What if you don't like it, Mom? What if you don't like the food?"

"I'll like it," she says.

On Friday, I put a few suitcases in the car and drive my parents over. Mommy and I have a new bed and a small kitchen table delivered from Raymour & Flanigan. Until the rest of their furniture comes, it is all they have. When we arrive, we walk through a communal living area, where people are watching an old Bogart movie on a big-screen television. We walk by a grand piano, through a dining area, past a little store and two caged mynah birds, to the first-floor apartment. It is pretty. There is a bedroom with a big double window, a nice-size bathroom with a new floor, and a living room/kitchenette with French doors that go out to a pretty patio on a communal garden. You can't hear the sound of Highway 434 at all, even though it is adjacent to Castle Gardens. They got one of the best apartments in the whole place and it is affordable, too. Just $1,250 a month, with meals and some housekeeping included.

Yet something is wrong. I realize I have become upset. Something feels terrible inside me. I am not sure why.

I tell myself that it will be okay, Daddy will adjust to this. I will adjust. Ava will adjust. My mother will take good care of him. Although still weak, she seems more energetic now than when she first arrived.

My mother walks around the apartment. "This is perfect," she says. "This is just right. It is a lot like Encantalada."

Vista Encantalada is the place where my parents lived for a while in Albuquerque, after my mother stopped cooking. The apartment there had the same floor plan, with an additional small room.

Daddy suddenly remembers it. "This is exactly like that other place!" he says.

"It is really similar," Mommy says. "He is thinking of the balcony thing." Encantalada had a door to a patio, too.

Daddy takes my arm and gently pulls me out of the room into the hallway. He has something he wants to tell me.

"Is this okay?" I ask him. "Do you want to live here? Will you be comfortable here?" I ask.

My father looks at me hard, like he is trying to figure something out and is struggling. He looks right into my eyes.

"I am not sure who you are," he says, "or why you have been so nice to me, but I will tell you this: If I hadn't hooked up with that one in there"—he gestures with his thumb inside the apartment—"you would have made a great wife."

He smiles and puts his hand out to me. Unsure what to do, I take it.

We shake like businessmen, or people who have just struck a silent pact, a deal, and know that it means a change. There is no going back.

I can't help it, I am crying. I can't stop. I am like Daddy before he got Prozac. I feel like my insides are collapsing. My face is melting. The world seems impossible to live in. I pick up Ava and rush out of Castle Gardens before anyone can see me. She looks at me strangely and seems scared. "Mommy cryning. Mommy cryning," she says.

I wipe away my tears as best I can. I don't even say good-bye to my parents. I just left Daddy there with Mommy. She said she wanted to go to the pretty dining room to wait for dinner, even though it was only three o'clock. The people there say they can furnish the apartment temporarily. I have run away, leaving them alone in an empty apartment, before anyone has even brought in a chair.

Ava and I drive home alone. The car seems empty without Daddy, without his confusion and questions. Ava says, "Park, Mommy," and I pull over at her favorite playground. I am still crying. Tears are surging out from somewhere inside me I have never felt before. I am crying from a place I didn't know I had. It is a unique sensation.

I think about how to express it, how I could write a column

about the pain of leaving a parent in a place like that for the first time. About the sense of being left yourself, of loss.

I decide not to even try.

When we get out of the car Ava says, "No crying, Mommy!" and puts her arms around me. She kisses my cheek. Then she runs to the swings. I put her in one and push.

For a long time I stand there in the melting snow, pushing my daughter. Higher and higher. She likes it when I do, she leans back in the swing to face the sky. "Hi, sky," she says.

We are back to being two people again. Daddy is gone. I wonder what will become of us.

chapter 26

Large-Brained Animals

>———⊷———◆∞ ⊠ ∞◆———⊷———◉

S hane calls.

"Hi," he says.

"Hi."

"How is Ava?"

"Good. Big."

"I miss her. I miss you."

"She misses you, too. It has been a hard winter."

I decide to tell him something small and painful, a poison dart: "I gave back Franny."

"Listen, I am sorry. I messed up. I am not with Marty anymore."

I can't think of anything to say. All the words in my brain swim away from me, like startled fish. We are silent for a long time, which seems stupid.

"Listen, Elizabeth," Shane says. "I want to come home."

Ohmygod. This I hadn't thought of. This I do not need.

· · ·

The problem with being abandoned is not the abandonment itself. That softens with time, you figure out ways to cope.

I decided early this year that evolutionary biologists had it all wrong. The reason humans evolved is neither our large brains nor our opposable thumbs. It is our coping skills. As a species, we know how to deal.

Think of the Holocaust. Think of the Japanese internment camps. Think of the packs of orphans in Brazil, who scavenge through garbage for food and grow to adulthood on street corners. Think of people in trees in Mozambique.

I think of my mother. She coped with my father's forgetting for years, turning it into something it wasn't. Out of her love and need for him, she made it into an asset, like his great intellect, his fine work as an arbitrator and professor. He had a great forgettery. She decided he was so brilliant he didn't have time to notice details, like directions, names, places, specifics. It used to anger me. It doesn't anymore. I see it for what it is now. We all have to deal with things in our own way.

The problem with being abandoned, I decide, is that sometimes the abandoner decides to come back.

⸺◈ ⋇ ◈⸺

It has been a few weeks, and every day my mother calls. She updates me with reports on the place they are living and all its inadequacies. "We have to move," she says.

She tells me things are strange at Castle Gardens. People die and are taken away, but she never sees any ambulances. "I think they come and get them at night when we are all asleep. It's creepy."

Someone has told me that Castle Gardens was the name of

the point of entry to the United States, before the opening of Ellis Island. It is an interesting choice for the name of a senior living facility. A lie, really. All those people, starting a new life in America, passed through the historic Castle Gardens. The people who pass through this Castle Gardens are not starting lives. If anything, they are finishing. Their lives are over, and now they are treading water, waiting.

Mommy is upset that they post the names of the dead on a bulletin board above the place where they have posted pictures of her and my father and the other new residents. "They are old people, Mom," I say. "Some of them are going to die."

"I know that," she says. "But it is the way they die. So quietly."

She tells me that is not the main reason she wants to move. The main reason is the food. "It's usually cold. And they rarely put any salt or bread on the tables."

It is my birthday. Someone gives me a certificate for an "afternoon of beauty." I sit in a chair at the salon getting my eyebrows waxed. "You have a few grays here," the technician points out. "It's funny, they are only on the left side. You want a tint?"

She tells me that she can dye my eyebrows black, it will give me a more "defined look."

I look in the handheld mirror she holds up and see it. Sure enough, my left eyebrow is aging. "Sure," I say. "I'll take a tint."

I think a few years ago I might have been concerned about my appearance, with graying left eyebrow hairs at forty-one. I might have thought about the end of my youth, the onset of middle age. But now another thought pops up. I wonder if somewhere in my head, corresponding to the seven gray eye-brow hairs, are seven neurons, being squeezed to extinction by a beta-amyloid cluster. Or seven beta-amyloid clusters, about to march across the plains of my brain, filling the gray matter with their sticky bounty, and knocking out my memories, one by one.

Coping. I am coping. I am getting better at it all the time.

chapter 27

Labor in the United States

———⟨∞ ⅱ ∞⟩———

It is July and *Time* magazine has published their own cover story on Alzheimer's. I figure the editors there thought enough time had gone by since the January *Newsweek* report for it to have some newsstand appeal.

What is nice about the *Time* report is that it departs from the crisis motif and focuses on hope, prevention, and cure. On the cover it says "The New Science of Alzheimer's." Below there are bullet points: The drugs, the genetics, the latest theories, and "what you can do now." I grab it greedily off the rack at the drugstore. I want to know what I can do now.

The long and short of it is there are really smart people chasing down the causes of the disease, and they are getting very close. Beta amyloids, they've discovered, are just proteins. Simple proteins that have mutated out of control. They were first seen in 1906 by a German neuropathologist named Alois Alzheimer as he looked through a microscope at tissue from the brain of a patient named Auguste D., a woman who got angry and paranoid and seemed to think other people were extensions of herself.

In the 1980s, researchers identified a gene—chromosome 21—that contains the encoded information for making the out-of-whack proteins. They located early-onset genes, too, Presenilin 1 and 2. They were the ones who identified the four-thousand-member Colombian family that was "haunted for generations" by Alzheimer's, leading them to the foregone conclusion that the early-onset variety, while by far the rarest, could run in families.

In the research community, a war has broken out between the amyloid people and the APOE4 people, who say that the genes are just "susceptibility factors." They say the lipoprotein called APOE4 is the real culprit. In other words, people with the marked genes are at a higher risk but will not invariably develop the disease. Furthermore, there could be other genes bearing such susceptibility markers, like a gene called A2M on chromosome 12.

What is good about the war between the amyloid people and the APOE4s is that they are racing against each other. Their competition fuels faster research, good news for those of us who could have ticking genes and either lipoprotein or beta amyloids poised to abduct our memories forever.

In California last year, the amyloid people genetically engineered mice to develop amyloid plaque. Then they vaccinated baby mice against it and the plaque dissolved.

This should be good news, I should celebrate the curing of these mice. It should buoy me on a raft of hope. But I can't help it, it just makes me laugh. I laugh hard like Ava, until my side aches, but then I can feel the laughter moving dangerously near that crying place. It is so sad and funny. All those research mice, in danger of forgetting their cages, their running wheels, the beautiful sensation of chomping down on a piece of grade-A Wisconsin cheddar.

For mice, at least, the problems of forgetting is on the verge of being solved.

I think about writing a letter to Elan Pharmaceuticals offering myself up as research fodder. I will be the first human subject to take the amyloid vaccine. I will be their amyloid crash-test dummy. I would offer them Daddy, but I am sure it is too late.

The *Time* story includes a simple test you can give yourself, not unlike the Mini-Mental State Exam. This time, I take it. I count backward from twenty, I say the months backward, and I remember the phrase *John Brown, 42 Market Street, Chicago.* I know the year and month and the time of day.

Good for me, I say. I mentally pat myself on the back. I am just fine. But then I get depressed. The test asks how the test taker has been doing writing checks, paying bills, assembling tax records, and working on hobbies. Since Daddy came, last summer, I have written about fifteen checks. Bill collectors call me daily. My tax records are a shambles. As for my only real hobby—quilting—I haven't even gone near my quilting basket this year.

But it's okay. So far I have not worn my bathrobe to the park, something *Time* says could signal the onset of stage 1 of the disease. I do not even know where my bathrobe is anymore.

When I read the section on "what caregivers can do," I feel a real sense of accomplishment. Much of what they suggest, I have done. Over the winter I made signs, labeled drawers, and put up calendars and clocks. I made places—what they call "orientation areas"—for Daddy to keep things. I encouraged him to get out, to go to class, and to go on all those walks in Cole Park he so despised. I tried not to "correct" Daddy's faulty memories.

In the last stage of Alzheimer's—stage 3, "severe," when the patient cannot eat or swallow, dress, bathe, or groom himself and has trouble with bladder and bowel function—the article says caregivers should minimize pain from unnecessary blood tests and other procedures and "try to communicate in a different way, through exchange of photos or through music."

As Daddy moves closer to that place, I have put pictures of us everywhere. I have ripped them out of albums and frames. I have photocopied them and taped them to the walls at Castle Gardens. I have bought CDs of big-band music, Ella Fitzgerald, Frank Sinatra, and the Beatles. Once I put them on, he stands up and reaches for my mother or me.

He wants to dance.

It has been a cool summer, rarely above seventy-five degrees. This is a good thing for both my parents. They have not had to experience those stifling East Coast days, when the hot, humid air feels like it cannot fit into your nose. They have had mild weather in which to get accustomed to their new lives at Castle Gardens, where they remain. My mother says she is losing weight. She can't eat the Castle Gardens food. She calls their meatballs "cannonballs" and she says the steaks "are just like rubber."

She has a lot of complaints. Sometimes she even hints she'd like to move back here, with us. Ava and I spend a lot of time with them, sitting in their tiny living room or out on their little porch. She likes to take my mother's flowerpot off its stand and turn the stand upside down. Then she sits on it.

Ava and I go to the park a lot now. At twenty-two months, she is old enough and coordinated enough to go down even the tallest twisty slide by herself. In fact she insists on it. She is fearless, goes on her tummy headfirst or lies down on her back. She likes the thrill. She loves slides and swings. But above all other things on earth—with the exception of myself, her Pop-pop, and Elmo—she loves sandboxes. Sometimes at night she talks about sandboxes in her sleep. When she wakes up, it is her first thought of the day.

"Sanbox?"

Sometimes I bring my parents with us to the park and they watch her slide and swing and dig in the sand with me. They sit on a park bench next to the playground equipment and smoke.

Ava and I go to Cole Park now for a different purpose than our walks of the fall, winter, and spring. We go to swim in the lake. She loves it when I hold her by the arms and twirl her around me in the shallow swimming area for children. " 'Gain! 'Gain! 'Gain!" she demands.

When she is exhausted from swimming and digging holes in the sand, she falls asleep on a blanket I spread on the lake's soft white beach.

When Shane came home in early June, after nearly nine months away, Ava surprised us both. She saw him walk in and glanced cavalierly up at his face. "Hi, Daddy," she said.

Then she ran into the hallway where there is a stack of his paintings and got one. She pulled it after her—not an easy task, it is bigger than she is—and handed it to him. "Daddy painting," she said. She remembered him.

It was more than I could say for myself. He has been gone from October to June, almost enough time to have a child, and when he walked in the door he looked strange somehow. I didn't recall that his hair was such a light color, like yellow cloth that has been washed many times. I had forgotten about those blue eyes verging on green. I had resigned myself to his absence. I had incorporated it and let go of the details of him. I let them drift out to the forgetting place where Daddy's mind has gone. I did it intentionally, maybe to punish him. Or to survive.

Now I do not know how to get those exiled feelings back. There is no clear road to them. I would have to start from the beginning, get to know him from scratch. The winter was so multilayered, so thick with struggle, there is no way I can ever tell him about it. It will always be a membrane between us that cannot be crossed.

What has been interesting about Shane's return is that on a certain level I realize I would rather have my father come home. It was hard for me to admit this to myself. It feels like an unhealthy thing, to prefer your father to your husband. But it is true.

The meaning of family for me has shifted entirely. Now I think of family as the people who stick by you, the ones who are there when you go through things. For me, family has become a trajectory of Cohens: Daddy, me, and Ava. This mountain, this house, Samo and the cats, are a part of my family, too. Somewhere out there are the bears. The bears I have created, or sensed, or seen in the gray of dawn in shadows. They, too, are my family.

And I have learned something about myself I didn't know before. That what Mr. Wright once said is true. I am strong. I can take care of people.

I had always thought of myself as the one who needed to be cared for, and now that has changed. I do not want to go back to the way things were before.

But Ava does. For nearly nine months—half her life—after living with Daddy in rooms full of forgetting and loss, she re-membered.

I prayed nightly for her. I prayed for her chromosomes 21, 12, and for Presinilin 1 and 2; for her lipoproteins and proteins. I prayed that someday she will have memories of being swirled through lake water and buried in sandy beaches, twirling down slides, digging her toes into sandboxes, and being kissed by her mother while she slept. I prayed that she would always remem-ber her time with Pop-pop. And I prayed, hard, that she would never forget Shane. That her protean memory would hold on to this man who loved her in spite of the fact that he was gone.

And it had worked. She remembered.

———◆◆◇◆◇◆——

At first it was hard, feeling like Shane could belong here again. We had to talk and fight about it, to see if it was something that could even be possible. Ava's love for him, and his for her, is so clear and so real. It seems selfish to deny them each other. And I, too, still have feelings for him. He is the father of my child. He is the man who chose this house with me. The man who painted my grandmother and her sisters dancing, from an old photograph. He is the man I sat with in a hollowed-out canyon in New Mexico, one I considered my other self, my male self.

I know what I should tell him about our time apart, the things that happened here in the heart of winter, but I can't think of anything to say. "Sometime you can read my diaries," I say. "If you ever want to know."

He says he wants us to look forward instead of back. He will not read the diaries. "I had a terrible winter, too. I missed you both so much."

When he first went into his studio and saw the mess made by Samo those times I locked him in, he was angry and threw things. Then he cried for a long time. I could hear him in there. He brought out a shredded piece of a photograph. It was the only picture he'd had of his parents and him together. His father died in a car wreck when he was a teenager.

I have noticed that for certain things in life, apologies seem more like insults.

Jody wants to know if Shane is staying. She was uncomfortable around him at first, but she has eventually begun to warm up to him. He got a night job at the Hess gas station and sold a few paintings. He wants to contribute, to be a part of us again.

"I don't know what will happen," I tell Jody.

When he asks me one night if we could think about trying again, I say I do not know. He wants to know if I think we "will work out ultimately."

What is ultimately? I ask.

Until we begin to forget each other's names? Until we forget the names of trees? The seasons? The days of the week? Or until we are buried like the people in the cemetery across the road? Until we are names on stones that people will read and puzzle over, trying to fit into a story, an arc of a life?

I try to tell him about the small pocket of time between remembering and forgetting, how fragile it is, but I can see he thinks I am going off on a tangent.

I tell Shane I sometimes count the days I have left until I forget everything. I figure I have 11,920 days until all names, facts, dates, and other information are exiled to my forgettery. I have seen how it happens. Things begin to sift away, they leave you.

He says that is crazy. "You don't know what will happen in the future," he says.

"My point exactly," I say.

Shane takes my father to get ice cream and my mother to dinner at the Olive Garden and Red Lobster. He says he wants to help her get her strength back. At our house he mows the lawn and plants several hundred bulbs, "so the spring will be gorgeous."

"I don't see why we can't still have a great love," he says. He wants to know if I can forgive and forget. I tell him forgiving is no problem. I am pretty sure I can do that. What he doesn't understand is that forgetting is my enemy. I cling to details like a life raft. I do not want to let go of anything. My greatest fear is if I let go just a little each day I'll wind up like Daddy, and I won't know Ava's name when I am eighty.

I want to know Ava's name forever.

My mother calls a lot now. She asks me to take her places, buy her things. She buys me things, too. A new bed. New mattresses. A new black purse. She asks me to get a beeper so she can contact me at any time. "It would make me feel less uneasy," she says.

Then she calls me one morning. "Come and get Daddy, I can't do this," she says. "He's an idiot."

I drive over with Ava and Shane.

My mother is furious. She says she isn't speaking to my father. "I ask him to close a window and he brings me a hairbrush. I ask him for a glass of water, he turns on the television."

I can only think of one solution for her. "Don't ask him for things," I say.

"Don't be smart with me," my mother says.

"Mom, Daddy has Alzheimer's disease. He always will. This is the way things will be from now on. And maybe worse."

She starts crying. "Why are you telling me this? You want to break my heart. You enjoy it."

We take Daddy back. He is very confused in the car. "You know, for the life of me I can't figure out what I have done to make that woman so mad at me! I try to be so nice to her all the time."

When we get to our house he says, "This old place! I lived here for years with my daughter. How is it holding up? People still live up here?"

"I live here, Daddy," I say. "I am that daughter. We lived here last winter with Ava and Samo and the cats. You got lost once in the snow."

"I did!" he says. "I remember that. I couldn't find my way back."

I feel a sense of minor victory. He remembers our house. It is a remarkable thing, and it tells me he is still in "stage two of the disease, moderate." During stage 2, *Time* magazine said, the afflicted can still process some new information. He "processed" the house, his daughter, the winter storm. But he is unclear why Shane is here now.

"Why is that chap always hanging around?" he asks.

And more and more now his bowels are giving him trouble, a sign that stage 3 could be approaching. He asked my mother to find someone to help him shave.

"I am afraid about it," he told her. "It could be dangerous."

I had always hung on to his shaving as a sign of wellness, a skill like a healthy canary in a coal mine that is still safe.

We decide Daddy will come and stay with us on the weekends, to give Mommy a break. On Monday mornings he returns to Castle Gardens. Shane, meanwhile, has begun the task of remaking his studio on the first floor of our house. He is reclaiming territory, going through all the stuff the dogs destroyed.

I see him playing with the tiny people in the toy village again. He makes a skirmish. Men on horses are attacking men on foot, dressed like peasants. I cannot tell who wins.

I have to wonder what would have happened to us if Shane hadn't arrived, if my mother had stayed in Seattle. Would Daddy and Ava and I be okay? For some reason I picture us out in the field behind our house, dancing together, watching the butterflies catch onto the milkweed.

I see us happy.

Who knows if that picture is accurate. Still, there it is, framed on a mantelpiece in my mind. It stands there on the path that was not chosen for us.

This is my life now. I live with Ava, Shane, Samo, and three cats: Twy-twy, Milo, and mean kitty Lulu. Every week or so my father is here for a few days.

We run an ad in the paper, and people come and get the five kittens. Two young couples come and take two each. Last of all a little girl comes with her father and takes the little white one that Ava calls "babykitty."

Just like she looked for her father and grandfather, Ava still looks for the white kitten sometimes. She got really attached. I see her peeking under couches. "Babykitty?! Come!"

When my father stays here we still do our memory project. He tells me his memories, about the war, about his childhood, the blisters on his hands. Most of them I have heard before. My memory book is full of versions of the same memories. It is as if his life has been boiled down to these few, singular experiences, and they have come to stand for everything in between.

"Did I ever tell you I was kidnapped in Bolivia?" he asks me. "It was the damnedest thing."

Whenever I bring Daddy back to my mother after a few days, she coos and holds his hand, she gives him ear-hair trims and runs his baths. She hand-washes the stains out of his pants. They kiss.

For a few hours they are young lovers again. They become the parents I grew up with, shamelessly demonstrative. They pretend that everything is normal until something happens, like when Daddy wanders into the wrong apartment or can't zip up his pants.

I am finally doing it. I am reading Daddy's most famous book—*Labor in the United States,* the fifth edition. I have a vacation, so I decided to try it. It is almost September. I sit on the front porch while Ava naps, drink iced coffee, and plunge into the world in which he was an expert, labor law.

I am actually getting through it, although I admit it is slow and I take a lot of breaks. There are interesting parts on the history of slavery, indentured servitude, the New Deal, and how the major car companies like Ford and Chrysler had conditions that were so awful they forced workers to create labor unions. I like the part on strikebreaking in particular. It is the closest thing to exciting Daddy's thick prose has to offer. I don't know why I was so afraid to read it all these years.

I tell Daddy, "I am reading *Labor in the United States.* I am reading the fifth edition."

"What do you think?"

"I like it. It is interesting."

"That's good," he says. "I'm glad there's a copy still kicking around."

Like me, Ava has expanded her reading repertoire. She has moved on now from *Fluffy Bunny* and *Goodnight Moon* to such literary classics as *The Runaway Bunny, The Cat in the Hat,* and her many ABC books. She knows the alphabet to *k*—her favorite part is *efg*—and can count to ten. She sits in the backseat and sings to herself: 1,2,3,4,5,6,7,8,9,10 and "Twinkle, Twinkle, Little Star." She sits by herself and turns the pages of books and says words that explain the pictures. Just like my father.

Shane says he will not leave again, even if we get into a bad fight. Even if my father has to come back here and live forever. Even if he has to change my father's diapers or spoon-feed him or roll him around in a wheelchair.

But just in case, I order and pay for our winter's heating oil in advance. I look into getting a new roof put on the house and better storm doors. I order wood and ask it to be stacked right on the porch, where I can get it easily. In life you have to make things as easy as you can for yourself. You can't depend on others to do things for you. You can't take chances.

This is how I have become. I am ready.

While he was gone, Shane acquired a new hobby. He listens to audiobooks while he paints. His favorites are corny Westerns, read by people with fake Texas accents. His paintings have gotten bigger and busier than they were when he went away. Many have men and women holding babies in them. There is one where a man with a baby in a stroller points to the sky where there is a shooting star.

When I look at these paintings, I feel as though I am walking through a museum exhibit about our lives. Here is the way we want to be, we should be. Here is the ideal us that isn't. It seems so distant, but worth striving for somehow.

Regret, anger, and hate seem like such a waste of time, and we have so little time here in the remembered world. Those emotions peel away from me and leave me naked, feeling numb. When I look at Shane now I try to feel hopeful. I try to feel.

When Daddy was staying here for a few days in July, he saw Shane in the front yard, holding Ava. He came over to me and said, "Something important I just want to alert you about. That chap out there in the yard has our baby. You might want to keep an eye on him."

I told Daddy I would.

Janet, the director of Castle Gardens, asks me to come in and speak with her. When I get there she has a nurse assistant and a social worker with her in her office. I sit down in a chair by the door. She tells me they are worried about my parents. They are worried about my mother's medications. They are worried about Daddy.

"We need to move him into the stage-two dining hall," she says.

"What is the stage-two dining hall?"

"It is for people with a higher degree of need."

"Why?"

Janet tells me Daddy stole someone's Jell-O. When my mother doesn't keep an eye on him, she says, he sits at other people's tables and eats their food.

My mother has denied this. He doesn't even like Jell-O, she has pointed out.

"We want you to think about a higher level of care," Janet says. "For the future. We have an Alzheimer's unit."

I ask Janet if it is a lockdown unit. I have told my father I will never admit him to a lockdown unit. He asked me to shoot him in the head first.

"We prefer to call it 'secured,' " she says.

The director and aides are very calm. There is no getting around it, they say, Daddy is getting worse. Janet also says Daddy went into someone else's apartment and took a pillow.

Like my mother, I find myself suddenly doubting them. My

father has never picked up a pillow in his life. He is not a pillow-picking-up sort of man. All winter at my house, he never once picked up a pillow.

"Why would my father want a pillow?" I ask.

"We have seen it before," one of the aides says. Janet and the other aide nod solemnly.

Janet says, "People come in here at his level and they deteriorate rapidly. They can only stay on that plateau so long."

They tell me what he will soon be facing, the loss of motor ability, of the ability to feed himself, bathe himself, shave. "They don't just forget how to walk, they eventually forget how to breathe," the aide says, almost whispering, as though Daddy's fate were too terrible a thing to say out loud.

The director of Castle Gardens and her assistants want me to know these things.

I thank them.

———————◦◦H◦◦————————

I have finished *Labor in the United States*. The last section of the book is the part on Social Security and aging. While much of it is highly technical—about public policy, and mandatory retirement, and early retirement trends and benefits—some sentences seem almost prophetic. If you were to draw a line in Daddy's life as to when he seemed to change, it would be after his retirement. When Daddy stopped teaching at the university and doing his arbitration, he seemed to fade, as though without his work he had no real purpose, no identity.

Sanford Cohen was Sanford Cohen because he had great thoughts. He knew things and understood things most people didn't understand. He made decisions that companies abided by.

He graded exams and papers. Once he refused to grant a graduate student a Ph.D.

On page 449 of *Labor in the United States,* Daddy wrote:

> Many of the problems besetting the aged in our society have been intensified by various aspects of modern life. Along with the advances in medical science that have increased life expectancy, changes have occurred in our social and economic arrangements that, on the whole, make adjustments to the problems of old age more difficult. Our society, for example, has become less rural, more urban. On the farm, where economic activities are ordered around the family unit, the aged are able to contribute technical skill and know-how long after the decline in strength requires a tapering off of their physical contributions to the work. In the rural society, furthermore, the family usually consists of a large kinship group. The young, middle-aged, and old remain parts of an integrated economic and social unit in which status and privileges increase with age. . . .
>
> In modern urban life there has been a strong tendency for the family to become what sociologists call the extreme conjugal family type. When a male city dweller refers to his family he is usually referring to his wife and his children and not to his parents, brothers, or sisters. Old people have no definite claim upon an extended kinship group for support and social participation. . . .
>
> This means that people must depend more and more upon their own resources for psychological and economic security in their old age.

I read the end of the book at night, by the light of a small lamp next to the bed, while Ava sleeps beside me. She still sleeps with a pacifier. Occasionally, she takes it out and puts it in her ear, that old habit of hers from her bottle days. While I read, I unconsciously pull the binky out of her ear and brush aside a strand of hair from her face. She wakes and sits up. "More cup?" she says.

I get up to fill her sippy cup with water and she holds her arms up to me. "Me!" she says. Translation: Take me with you to the bathroom.

As I carry her in, she puts her head down on my chest, closes her eyes. I refill the cup with one hand, a complex maneuver, especially screwing and rescrewing the cup top. For a few seconds I sit her on the ledge of the sink.

While I am twisting the top back she looks up and sees her reflection in the mirror. "Hi, me; hi, Mommy," she mumbles.

When I put her down again, she sucks on the cup for a few seconds and shuts her eyes, one hand gripping the cover of the last edition of his textbook my father ever wrote. It was lying next to me on the bed.

She is a big girl now. I wonder if someday she will remember anything about this time we share that seems so nice to me. The duet of us, sleeping and dreaming side by side each night. The early mornings when we play. I have decided that on her second birthday she will start sleeping in her own room. I am fixing up the room at the end of the hall—Daddy's room—with Jody's help. We are filling it with pictures of Big Bird and Elmo and all her favorite things. I will lie in there with her for the first few nights. I will make sleeping in her own room a good thing, Ava's special place. I will miss her beside me, but it is time now.

On one wall I will hang a picture of Daddy and Ava together. In the picture he is holding her on his lap, and she's reaching out to touch his cheek. She is laughing at his prickly whiskers.

They say most people don't really recall much that happens before they are around four, so there is a chance she may never remember him, this winter of the three of us, of our lives on Beartown Road.

That is why I will hang the picture up. So she can always see him. I am hoping somewhere deep in the neurological structure of her brain she will retain a sharp orange flare of Daddy. The man who followed her around one winter and worried about her falling down the stairs. The man who built a fire to keep her warm when she was sick; who said, "Hi there, little guy," every time she entered a room. Who loved her so completely, although he never learned her name.

chapter 28

The Crossing Place

>——·—‹‹•⊹•››—·——‹

But he does remember.

He does.

I take Daddy back to Castle Gardens after a weekend at our house. When I come to see him the next day, he looks up from a semistupor. A strand of drool hangs from his lip like thread with a dewdrop at the bottom. He looks up and smiles. He takes my hand in his, which is shaking. And he says this: "Finally you are here. My daughter. Where on earth . . ."

"Have I been?" I finish for him.

"Where?"

I turn my head so he doesn't see me wipe the corners of my eyes.

At last. My father has learned me. He may not know me by name, but he knows me. He knows who I am. His daughter.

"Daddy, I've been working, taking care of the house, the dog, you know, the usual."

"Where are you . . . living now?"

"Up on the mountain, Daddy. You know, on Beartown Road."

Daddy can picture the house only if I say the word *mountain*.

"Still up there?" he asks. "How about that."

"Yup."

"What do you do up there?"

"Not much, the usual."

He still holds my hand in his. His hands are cold.

"And how . . ." He pauses, then asks, "about my little Ava?"

I turn away again, wiping tears. I look to see if anyone is around, if I alone have witnessed this miracle. Didn't anybody hear that? Didn't anybody hear that but me?

My father has invented fire.

He has mastered quantum physics.

He has learned my daughter's name.

"She is great, Daddy. Getting bigger."

"When you gonna bring her here? When can I see my little girl?"

Contrary to all the experts' predictions, contrary to the books and articles, the websites I've read and people I have spoken to, Daddy did it. He learned something.

They said it wasn't possible. That his brain was finished, he never would learn anything again. Daddy showed them.

I drive straight home to get Ava. When we get to Castle Gardens, she runs ahead of me. She pushes the special buzzer on the door to Special Needs, where Daddy was moved a month ago.

The aide comes and unlocks the door. Ava races into the dining area and leaps into Daddy's lap.

"Pop-pop!" she yells. "I love you. Big hug."

She still watches Teletubbies. She learned to say "big hug" from the show. She pulls his thumbs and makes him stand up. "C'mon, Pop-pop, come play Ava."

"Oh boy," he says. He is smiling. "Here we go."

Ava drags him down the halls and takes him into the television room, where she pushes the buttons on and off and changes the channels. She takes him into the bathroom and together they turn the toilet paper roll around and around, tearing off little pieces and throwing them in the garbage.

Then she drags him along to her favorite spot: Special Needs has a fish tank.

"C'mon, Pop-pop, help Ava see fish."

Daddy trails along as best he can. "I can't keep up!" he says. "Oh, she is getting so big."

In the presence of Ava, Daddy regains the ability to speak a complete sentence. After all, she can do it. For more than a month she has been talking nonstop in sentences. She talks about the mole on my neck, her tiny plastic horse that got flushed down the toilet, she talks about the moon and mean kitty Lulu.

On the bench in front of the fish tank, Ava sits on Daddy's lap, and over and over they say each other's names.

"Hi, Pop-pop."

"Hi, Ava."

"Pop-pop—hey!"

"Ava—hey!"

"Pop-pop, hi."

"Ava, hi."

. . .

The brain of my father and the brain of my daughter have crossed. On their ways to opposite sides of life, they have made an X. They look upon each other with fond familiarity. And they see each other heading to the place they have just come from. On his way out of this life, Daddy has passed her the keys.

Instead of thinking about him losing the abilities to speak, to walk, and to negotiate the world, I like to think he has given them to her.

Acknowledgments

During the time that the events in this book occurred I kept a diary. Woken frequently at night by my daughter and my father, I found myself sleepless, thoughts racing, and the computer became my destination. Soon, some of the words I was writing at night became the columns I was writing during the day for my job at a newspaper in Binghamton, New York. So it happened that Broome County began to share the story of my family. Not long after, the mail came in. All sorts of people who take care of other people wrote to me to say that I should not feel alone. The words of my readers were more than comforting, and for this I wish to thank them.

Caring at once for the elderly and very young, those of us in between, the so-called sandwich generation, can feel stuck, confused, exhausted, claustrophobic, and entirely blessed. Inside the embrace of generations we are surrounded by need, but also by love. This conundrum was appreciated by my editors at the *Press & Sun-Bulletin,* who allowed me to continuously dwell on the situation facing my own family on their pages. I thank them for that and also for giving me the flex time and leave needed to complete this book. Special gratitude goes to my managing editor, Gary Graham, and his wife, Jane, who were there throughout this process with encouragement, friendship, and emergency baby-sitting services.

I also wish to thank all those who were kind to our family. The Hackett and Lasky families, and especially Jody Hackett-Lasky, Dr. Frank Eder, Gene and Betty Wright, Tina "Ti-Ti" Hudock, "Grandma" Judy McDonald, Connie Nogas, and so many others—all of you who reached out to our family.

To my mother, Julia Cohen, and my sister, Melanie Thomas, goes my gratitude for trusting me to tell our family's story.

I have also been blessed with friends who were great solace during the writing of this book, especially Samme Chittum, Jenny Lyn Bader, David Margolick, and Julie Eisenberg.

To my agent David Black, who met me by telephone one afternoon and became an instant advocate, also goes my gratitude.

But writing this book would never have been possible without the vision, understanding, and compassion of Katie Hall. She is, without doubt, the hardest-working, most intuitive, devoted, and encouraging editor one could wish for.

Thank you to Kate Medina for believing in this book and in me.

The
Family on
Beartown Road

Elizabeth Cohen

An Interview:
Anna Quindlen and Elizabeth Cohen
Discuss *The Family on Beartown Road*

An Interview:
Anna Quindlen and Elizabeth Cohen
Discuss *The Family on Beartown Road*

————⫷◊◊⫶◊◊⫸————

Anna Quindlen, bestselling author of *Blessings* and *A Short Guide to a Happy Life,* recently sat down with Elizabeth Cohen to discuss what it was like to write *The Family on Beartown Road.*

Anna Quindlen: This book deals in part with your experience as part of the "sandwich generation," a generation of people simultaneously caring for their aging parents and their own young children. Could you speak to that issue a bit?

Elizabeth Cohen: When my father moved in with me I joined the growing ranks of the sandwich generation. Daily, we tend to the needs of people at the opposite ends of life, needs that sometimes mimic one another but also can clash. I have my own name for it; I call it "extreme parenting." In most cases the people in the middle of the sandwich generation have children who are school age or even about to go to college. Rarer are those who, like me, find themselves in the position of caring for an elderly, infirm parent or one with Alzheimer's disease at the same time they have an infant. That can mean feeding and diapering two very different sorts of people.

But there is a silver lining. When your parent and your child find a place where they can communicate with each other, when you see that they have begun to give each other some solace, it can be quite beautiful.

AQ: How is writing a memoir different from writing columns?

EC: Column writing is snapshot writing. You do not have the time or space to expound on anything, so you settle for a picture. You set a scene and communicate one or two ideas. You tell a story in brief. In a memoir you have the space to spread your thoughts out. To decorate them. To let them breathe and evolve and build.

AQ: Was it harder to write a memoir?

EC: It was different. Column writing can be very stressful because of the pressure of daily deadlines. Memoir writing is scary in a different way, because you become aware that your readership is so much larger and broader.

AQ: Do you feel as though writing this memoir changed you?

EC: The experience changed me. Being with my dad and daughter alone, responsible for them both, trying to meet their needs, made me grow up. I feel changed entirely. The parts of me that skirted responsibility, that took easy ways out, that opted for an extra ten minutes in bed in the morning, were voided. In their place came a person who grew the capacity to put herself on a shelf. I became much more patient. Writing the memoir became a release valve for all the pressures that built up.

AQ: This is a courageous work: you were all alone, you handled taking care of your father and your daughter, Ava, and you wrote a book.

EC: I felt very alone. I was scared of my situation, and writing about it seemed to help.

AQ: Usually when I've written quite personally about a family or a friend, I can show them the material, or at least tell them what I'm doing so they can approve. But with your father, who had Alzheimer's, and your daughter, who was only a toddler, you couldn't do that.

EC: The ethical questions loom large for me. Is it right to write about people whom you cannot ask for permission? I don't know.

AQ: Do you have a shortstop in your writing? In other words, are there privacy boundaries you won't cross in telling the story of your life? I know in my own life, writing about my kids and family, I reached a point where it no longer felt appropriate to keep writing about their lives. I had to stop.

EC: I have no shortstop. And I have thought a lot about this. I did not stop myself from writing down absolutely anything and everything that happened to me during the time this book was written. Possibly that is because I didn't know I was writing a book at the time I began and then that tell-all style became my template for the later parts of the book, when I did know I was writing a book.

AQ: You have done a wonderful turn for your father, commemorating his life in this lovely book.

EC: I have thought about that a lot, too. This book depicts him at his weakest moment of life. He was and is truly a great man—he cared about people, he lived his life following strong ethical principles, he fought to help unionize the hospitals in Albuquerque, New Mexico, he fairly arbitrated for labor unions all over the country, he struggled to help find solutions for desperate economies in the Third World. It seems sad, too, that he may be remembered now for this disease that snatched him at the end of a remarkable and stellar life.

AQ: I am not sure that is how he'll be remembered. I think all that he was comes through. We get a feeling for who he was throughout his life, not just who he became. Especially in the part where you quote from his book at the end and talk about his work in economics. It is just sad he doesn't know about it.

EC: Well, he was always very proud of me for my writing, and although I can never know for sure, and I could not really ask him (although I tried), I believe he would have supported this project, even though it would reveal so much of the intensely private realm of his life.

AQ: One part of the book I love is when, as your father's mind wanders, he invents phrases, wonderful phrases, to express himself. Some of those were like poetry.

EC: Word salad. That is what it is officially called. When my father could not remember the correct words for things he would grope for a substitute and that is when he came up with these beautiful words and phrases. He called apples the magnificent crackly ones, he called Ava the beautiful little one and me the beautiful big one.

AQ: That is the one I was thinking of, that is so wonderful about Ava, about her coming into a room.

EC: He said she was the one who fills the room with hurricanes. He meant, I think, that she makes a huge mess wherever she goes.

AQ: Another part that was very touching was about your neighbors. You had not even known them, and they became such an important part of your existence, and the way they came to help you out and delivered food was very touching.

EC: When winter really came on I realized how fearfully unprepared for it I was. That was when my neighbors stepped in. Fortunately they dug us out numerous times. They became friends, almost like family.

AQ: In the midst of all that was going on in your life, where and how did you find the time to write a book?

EC: I wrote at night. My father would wake me up when he would wander around the house, or Ava would wake me up when she woke up, as babies often do, and I would find myself sleepless. So I'd go to the computer. And that is when the bulk of this material came spilling out of me.

AQ: Did it help you to write it down? Was it a relief?

EC: It was therapy. My computer was my therapist. I really believe I was able to cope with intensely difficult circumstances because of two factors—the levity and joy that Ava brought to my life and being able to write it all down.

AQ: Taking care of a person with Alzheimer's disease is renowned for its difficulty. One thing you seem to have learned is how to humor the person with the disease to protect them.

EC: Yes, rather than correcting or trying to reorient my father all the time when he became confused, which could be very upsetting to him, I learned how to play along and humor him. If he asked me when we were going to Ohio, for example, I would just say, "In a week or so," even though we were not going to Ohio.

AQ: What did you learn from this time of your life? Would you do anything different now?

EC: I learned that you must be prepared in life. I always keep a stack of dry wood on my porch now. I have a hurricane lamp ready to go with oil. I keep flashlights. If I could go back in time I would get better vehicles, a snowblower, a better shovel. I would take more time with my father than I did then to savor his memories, his personhood, because time is harsh. Now he is almost completely gone. He no longer talks. He no longers sees me. I miss him even in the fractured state that he was in during the time of this book. I miss him so terribly. And there is no going back.

AQ: In a sense writing is all about memory, and your book is about memory being lost. Do you think that writing a book like yours staves off the loss of memories in some sense?

EC: There is no staving off the end of life, no staving off the end of memory; it runs its own course in each individual life. What you can do is save things for future generations. My sister recently said to me that she thought of this book as a gift for the children of our children and their children, etc. "What do we know about our great-grandmothers?" she asked me. We know nothing at all. Now a slice of time has been preserved for those future generations, if they are interested. And in a way it is good that it was a difficult time. It is really what a part of our lives were like.

AQ: In the book you worry a lot about losing your own memory. Do you still worry about that?

EC: Less now that my father lives separately from me. I still catch myself panicking sometimes when I lose the car keys or can't remember a name. But there is a calm I find now, too, when I need it.

Eventually we all lose our memories. Eventually we all become memories. All we have for sure is this moment now, and whatever we can summon in our hearts and minds about moments past. There is no guarantee that you can hold on to those. I see the world now in terms of memorable and nonmemorable things. Things that stay and things that blow past you without leaving anything behind. These are thoughts I never even had before I lived with my father on Beartown Road. These sorts of things never occurred to me.

Resource Guide
for People Caring for Individuals
with Alzheimer's Disease

Alzheimer's Association
www.alz.org
800-272-3900

A national network of chapters and the largest national voluntary
organization dedicated to helping families, the Alzheimer's Association
works to advance research and provide support to caregivers. Has
awarded more than $140 million in research grants.

Safe Return bracelet program
www.alz.org/resourcecenter/programs/safereturn_form.htm

A national program that distributes bracelets to Alzheimer's patients,
inscribed with a 24-hour-a-day, 800-number safety hotline, in case
they become lost.

Benjamin B. Green-Field Library and Resource Center
www.alz.org/resourcecenter/programs/libraryservices.htm
225 North Michigan Avenue
Suite 1700
Chicago, IL 60601-7633
800-272-3900

Part of the national Alzheimer's Association, this is the nation's largest library referencing materials dealing with Alzheimer's Disease. Information from the library can be obtained via phone, by e-mail, or in person. E-mail greenfield@alz.org with queries.

Artists for Alzheimer's
www.thehearth.org/artistsforalzheimers.htm

An organization providing volunteer musicians, painters, storytellers, and other artists who devote time and energy toward the improvement of the lives of people with Alzheimer's disease.

Fisher Center for Alzheimer's Research Foundation
www.alzinfo.org
800-ALZINFO

A New York University research program devoted to discovering the "cause, care and cure" for Alzheimer's disease. Provides caretaker families and individuals with savvy advice on medical help, pharmaceutical options, research updates, and information on how to sign up for clinical trials. Useful FAQs and tips on website.

AlzheimerSupport.com
www.alzheimersupport.com

Academic articles, research abstracts, links to support networks, legal information, chat room, and resources for caregivers. Plus a useful tip of the day.

Alzheimer's Disease Education and Referral (ADEAR) Center
www.alzheimers.org
PO Box 8250
Silver Spring, MD 20907-8250
800-438-4380

Organization culls National Institutes of Health information on the disease and catalogs resources. Offers useful books and will send out free pamphlets on aspects of the disease to caregivers and families.

United States Administration on Aging Eldercare Locator
www.eldercare.gov
800-677-1116

Free online and telephone assistance for locating help for the elderly.

About the Type

This book was set in Bembo, a typeface based on an old-style Roman face that was used for Cardinal Bembo's tract *De Aetna* in 1495. Bembo was cut by Francisco Griffo in the early sixteenth century. The Lanston Monotype Machine Company of Philadelphia brought the well-proportioned letter forms of Bembo to the United States in the 1930s.